D0124816
W9-BQS-109

How to Forgive

When You

Can't Forget

Healing Our Personal Relationships

CHARLES KLEIN

BERKLEY BOOKS, NEW YORK

HOW TO FORGIVE WHEN YOU CAN'T FORGET

A Berkley Book / published by arrangement with
Liebling Press, Inc.

PRINTING HISTORY
Liebling Press edition published 1995
Berkley trade paperback edition / October 1997

All rights reserved.
Copyright © 1995 by Charles Klein.
Text design by Jill Dinneen.
This book may not be reproduced in whole or in part,
by mimeograph or any other means, without permission.
For information address: Liebling Press, Inc.,
2971 Bellmore Avenue, Bellmore, New York 11710.

The Penguin Putnam Inc. World Wide Web site address is
http://www.penguinputnam.com

ISBN: 0-425-16004-1

BERKLEY®
Berkley Books are published by The Berkley Publishing Group,
a division of Penguin Putnam Inc.,
375 Hudson Street, New York, New York 10014.
BERKLEY and the ''B'' design
are trademarks belonging to Penguin Putnam Inc.

PRINTED IN THE UNITED STATES OF AMERICA

10   9   8   7   6   5

"I hope that many people find [this book], read it, and act on its suggestions."

> —Harold Kushner, *New York Times* bestselling author of *When Bad Things Happen to Good People* and *How Good Do We Have to Be?*

"A warm, wise, and wonderful message straight from the heart of God. It's one book I'll not only read, I'll reread and urge my friends to do likewise."

> —Robert H. Schuller, author of *You Can Become the Person You Want to Be*

"[This book] leads us on a path to true peace and healing. Charles Klein's wisdom has helped me and my family."

> —Bernie Siegel, M.D., *New York Times* bestselling author of *Peace, Love, and Healing*

"You can read it in one night but it will be helpful for a lifetime."

> —Rabbi Elliot Salo Schoenberg, The Rabbinical Assembly

"What a wonderfully wise book this is! This is a book we all need to read because all of us need to learn how to forgive if we are to live without rancor or resentment."

> —Rabbi Gilbert S. Rosenthal, The New York Board of Rabbis

"I found this book to be thought provoking, challenging, and practical in offering suggestions."

> —Brother William J. Martyn, S.A., Archdiocese of New York

Most Berkley Books are available at special quantity discounts for bulk purchases for sales promotions, premiums, fund-raising, or educational use. Special books, or book excerpts, can also be created to fit specific needs.

For details, write: Special Markets, The Berkley Publishing Group, 375 Hudson Street, New York, New York 10014.

Acknowledgments

The author is grateful for permission to reprint and adapt selections from the following:

"A Time to Forgive, But Never Forget" by Jay Feldman, a writer now living in California.

The Glory of Love, by Billy Hill. Copyright © MCMXXXVI Shapiro, Bernstein & Co., Inc., New York. Copyright Renewed. All Rights Reserved. International Copyright Secured. Used By Permission.

Permission granted by Ann Landers and Creators Syndicate to reprint articles from her syndicated column.

Acknowledgments

Material excerpted from *What a Funny Way to Say "I'm Sorry!"* Copyright © 1986 by Judith Viorst. Originally appeared in *Redbook*.

In addition, the author would like to thank Rabbi Moses A. Birnbaum, Larry King, Rabbi Harold Kushner, Rabbi Gilbert S. Rosenthal, Rabbi Elliot Salo Schoenberg, Rev. Robert Schuller, Dr. Bernard Siegel, and Oprah Winfrey for their help in bringing this book to the public's attention.

Liebling Press, Inc., would like to thank the following people who have provided endless support and encouragement: Betty Hesney, Jerry Seinfeld, Seena Kagan, Edward Liebling, Joshua Kal, Dr. Deborah Jean, Dan Strone, Sam and Sherry Husney, Elizabeth Barad, Lori Jonas and Ken Husserl. Thanks also to Kathy Anderson and Jean Schroeder of BookCrafters.

To my wife, Betty, and our children,
Joshua, Barry, Naomi, and Avram

And to my parents,
Doris and Martin Klein

In Appreciation

This book was written during my Sabbatical leave from the Merrick Jewish Centre. Away from my normal congregational responsibilities, I was able to focus on the book's development. I am grateful for the opportunity my congregation gave me during this time. Perhaps, even more important, I am deeply appreciative of the understanding, enthusiastic support and devotion that my congregation has shown me throughout the years.

I am indebted to Larry and Carolyn Liebling of Liebling Press, Inc. When they learned some time ago that I had a typed manuscript of this text sitting on my bookshelf, they encouraged me to bring its message to a wider audience. They cheered me on, believing in what this book says. I will be forever grateful for their guidance and unceasing support of this project.

The frenetic pace of my rabbinical work, which takes me

in so many directions, could not be managed without the concern and assistance of my secretary and friend, Pearl Kogan. She typed and then retyped this manuscript until we believed we finally got it right.

A special thanks to Diane Schoenberg. She edited this book with professional tenacity. She made sure that its message was clear and concise. Her efforts are gratefully appreciated.

And, as my tradition says, "last and most beloved," how thankful I am to my wife, Betty, and our children, Joshua, Barry, Naomi, and Avram. The children understood and adapted to the long periods of seclusion in my study. Betty's insights, delicate suggestions, and tactful comments challenged me, refined my thinking, and—ultimately—significantly improved the form and substance of this book. I am thankful for every day we share and for her love and support, which inspires everything I do.

Contents

Contents

INTRODUCTION:

Why a Book About Forgiveness

As colleagues, congregants, and friends came to learn that I had written a book about forgiveness, I found myself repeatedly answering the same question: Why forgiveness? That is, why would I write a book whose sole purpose is to motivate people to bring forgiveness into their lives? The answer is that I felt I had to write it. I had to find a way of making the message of this book available to the increasing number of people who live in the shadows of shattered relationships.

This book was written for the people whose stories I have heard over the years. It is for siblings who are no longer speaking, for children who have discarded their parents, and for parents who have severed all ties with their sons and daughters. It is also for grandparents who are cut off from life with their grandchildren because of problems with their own children. This book was written for all these people and others who will not know inner peace until they find a way back to the people they loved.

I have discovered that few families have been spared the pain of estrangement. Far too many experience this pain and have lived with it far too long. The message of this book is that the pain they know need not last forever. At some point, the anger and disappointment that separate us can yield to forgiveness. Even as painful memories linger on, we can still find our way back to those who were part of our lives.

You can forgive even when you can't forget. And only you can answer the age-old question, "If not now, when?"

There is a story told about a painter whose latest work was being unveiled before a gathering of art critics. They were scrutinizing the painting when one critic noticed what he felt was a glaring oversight by the artist. He called out, "Sir, I see that the door to the house in the painting has no handle. Was that deliberate?" The painter responded, "The door is the human heart. And there's no handle because it can only be opened from within."

How to Forgive When You Can't Forget

Healing Our Personal Relationships

CHAPTER I

Where Once There Was Love

> "Humanity is never so beautiful as when forgiving another."
>
> —Jean Paul Richter

H aving taken a seat on the train, I was just beginning to read my newspaper when I was recognized by the person sitting next to me. He was a friend of a member of my congregation and a frequent visitor to our synagogue. I wanted to read the paper, but he had an unstoppable need to talk to someone.

For the duration of our trip to Pennsylvania Station, he told me the story of his estrangement from his son and grandchildren. Although he had tried hard to be a good father and a caring grandfather, he suddenly and unexplainably was cast out of their lives. The granddaughter, whose college tuition he had paid when his son was out of work, was to be married and he was not invited to attend the wedding.

My fellow traveler desperately wanted to understand what had caused this rupture in his family. But every effort he made to reach out to his son went unanswered. Just when he thought he would be experiencing the joy of watching his grandchildren go on to the next stage of their lives, he found himself struggling to cope with the hurt he was feeling. His son and grandchildren were lost from his life and he needed someone with whom he could share his pain and tell of the betrayal he had suffered.

It troubled me to realize that this man's experience was not unique. In a world that wounds so many of us, people are searching for someone who will listen to and understand their pain. Often, in the most unlikely places, congregants and members of my community will turn to me, hopeful that I can give them a few moments of my time. My family is accustomed to the fact that a trip to almost anywhere will usually find me speaking with people who want to talk about their troubles, their worries, and their heartaches.

I've frequently heard people speak of the misery and desperation that comes when someone lives in the shadows of a shattered relationship. Through the conversations I've had over the years, I have come to know the special torment of those who yearn to see precious relationships restored. Their stories and their questions speak of their hurt. Uncertain and unhappy, they ask, "How can I take a person back into my life who has betrayed me?" Others who have sought forgiveness, only to be turned away, ask, "What do I have to do to show I'm sorry?" They want to know, "What will it take to bring us together again?" And most importantly, they wonder, "How long can this go on? How long can there be no forgiveness?" Their questions, their tears, and their pleas for help are evidence that above all, they want wholeness in their lives once again. They await forgiveness, hoping that it will lead to reconciliation and reunion.

Over the years, I've brought the message of forgiveness

and reconciliation to my congregation many times. And no matter how often I speak about the need to restore wholeness through forgiveness, I can see from the faces of my congregants that these words continue to touch and haunt them. I see it in the gentle poking that goes on during my sermon. I see it in the eyes that silently say, "Rabbi, you spoke about what pains me most of all." Some whisper, "Can I have a copy of your sermon? I want to send it to a member of my family." Others simply grasp my hand and ask that I reserve time for them in the coming week.

The tears, the whispers, the calls, the talks—they tell me, as they do every colleague I know, that among the most painful losses in life is the loss people feel when once cherished bonds have become severed.

Life for many families is far removed from what we see depicted on television during the holiday season. The warm family scenes do not necessarily capture the reality of family life. In too many homes, there are empty places at the holiday table. There are sons and daughters, brothers and sisters, mothers and fathers, and husbands and wives for whom holidays and every day are lived with an almost unbearable feeling of loss. Living hurts and celebration is unachievable when a relationship has been broken.

One popular television show recently devoted a program to the theme of reconciliation between adult children and their parents. Children who had not seen their parents for years told of their heartache. One after another, they introduced themselves and spoke in the hope that an estranged parent might hear their words on national television. Their pleas were heartrending. "Dad, if you're out there, I forgive you—I love you." "Dad, if you're listening, I don't care what happened so long ago—I just want to see you again." "Mom, I know

3

that we've had our differences, but we haven't seen each other in such a long time. I don't want to lose you forever.'' One young woman said, ''Mom, I know that there have been lies. I know that I have told you lies. But the pain I feel is no lie and the love I feel is no lie. Can't we get back together?''

It is not surprising that this program was broadcast just prior to the season of the year in which both Chanukah and Christmas are celebrated. Holidays and holy days are times when separation is most painful, when reconciliation is most desired, and when forgiveness is most obtainable.

I recall an experience I had in my first year of rabbinical studies in Jerusalem. As the students were preparing for Yom Kippur, the Jewish Day of Atonement, they began to place little notes on the bulletin board, asking the forgiveness of anyone they may have hurt or offended during the year just past. The messages were simple, but they created an atmosphere in which forgiveness and reconciliation were possible.

In the Jewish tradition, it long ago became the custom to turn to one another during the time of the High Holy Days and seek forgiveness from family members, friends, neighbors, and colleagues. I'm told that it was not uncommon in the synagogues of Eastern Europe to see people go around and quietly ask the forgiveness of fellow congregants and friends. Touched by this special spirit, the house of worship was transformed into a sanctuary of peace.

I have often used the days preceding Rosh Hashanah and Yom Kippur to work at healing troubled relationships. The undeniable emotional power of these holy days has frequently served as the catalyst for forgiveness. There have been times when I've spent the last few moments prior to the beginning of Yom Kippur bringing members of my congregation into my study, hoping that the highly charged atmosphere of this most sacred of days might motivate them to reconcile.

MOUNTAINS IN TIME

Holidays and holy days are mountains in time. They are moments when some are able to acquire a deeper understanding of life and what life requires of us. The special times of celebration that occur throughout the year on all religious calendars have the power to become life-transforming moments.

As we climb above the clamor and pettiness of daily life, we reach a vantage point from which life is viewed differently. We can see how many irreplaceable hours are spent nursing grievances. Perched upon these mountains, we often become wiser. Insults, disappointments, and hurts we've suffered appear smaller. These sacred times are the substance of life. They teach us, as Benjamin Disraeli said, that "life is too short to be small." From the top of these mountains, we see more clearly that life is too short to be unforgiving.

It was William Blake who wrote that "great things happen when men and mountains meet." If that mountain is a mountain in time, then our encounter has the potential of uplifting us, transforming us, and bringing something great and wonderful into our lives.

For some, the transforming moment is not a time of holiday celebration. It can be a period of illness or even a terrible tragedy. In the summer of 1989, a horrible airplane crash occurred in the cornfields of Iowa. Remarkably, there were many who survived. The gripping stories of those who faced death for the final 41 minutes of that flight were collected by *Life* magazine.

The survivors of Flight 232 found their 41 minutes of peril to be a mountain in time. They were asked what went through their minds during the minutes preceding the crash. Those who walked out of the wreckage had experienced something which cleared their vision. Perhaps, they better understood that above all, truly loving people means being forgiving and understanding. One traveler said that her life had changed. She experienced a great awakening—as if her point of reference had been transformed. With this dramatic shift, she came to regard trivial things truly as trivial. To her, fights and arguments all become unimportant.

When you realize that the sum total of the rest of your life may be lived in the next 41 minutes, you understand that "life is too short to be small." There are issues, incidents, hurts, betrayals, treasons, annoyances, and bruises which you have to put aside. Unless we do, we will waste precious, irreplaceable hours and opportunities.

And yet, there are people who will carry anger, disappointment, and their stories of betrayal and never put them down. Recently, a member of my congregation told me of a dispute she had been having with her husband for many years. A long time ago, their daughter had embarrassed them both. The daughter had made certain accusations and had deeply offended them. At the time, the three of them swore that they would never speak again. The father vowed that he never wanted to see his daughter.

With the passage of some time, the mother found a way to forgive. She explained to her daughter the hurt that she felt. And her daughter expressed her regret over the incident. But even as the mother had found a way to heal the hurt, the father continued to reject any communication with his daughter. He carried the anger and refused to forgive. The wife sat in my study and sobbed. She and her husband were growing older. All she wanted was for her husband to put down the hurt long enough to follow her and walk the path of forgiveness. Sadly, he continues to retell the story of his daughter's betrayal and has never forgiven her.

A BIBLICAL RECONCILIATION

One of the most poignant stories of forgiveness is found in the Book of Genesis. There we learn of the lonely childhood of Joseph, the son of Jacob. Joseph was surrounded by brothers who despised him. As the years went by, his brothers' hatred grew. Their hostility was so intense that some of his brothers even urged that they kill him. Reluctantly, they dissuaded themselves from taking his life and decided instead to get rid of Joseph by selling him to a passing caravan on its way to Egypt.

From that point on, the Book of Genesis describes Joseph's rise to power in Egypt. Recognizing Joseph's special talents, Pharaoh appointed him second in command over all Egypt, giving him the responsibility of preparing the country for the coming years of famine. When the famine came, its effect was felt over a wide area. Even Joseph's family who remained in Israel suffered from its devastation.

Having heard that there was food for sale in Egypt, Jacob sent his remaining sons to purchase provisions. When they arrived, the brothers were brought before the man in charge of food distribution. Unknowingly, they had come face to face with the brother they had sold into slavery many years before. Joseph recognized them. However, both the influence of Egyptian culture, along with the passage of time, had dramatically changed Joseph's appearance and his brothers failed to recognize him.

The narrative goes on to detail the elaborate scenario Joseph developed to see whether his brothers had changed during the 20 years that they had been separated from each other. As we follow the plot with its many turns, we sense that more is going on than meets the eye.

It has often occurred to me that as Joseph was putting his brothers to a test, he was also testing himself. Knowing that he had the power to avenge their treachery, it seems that Joseph was considering whether vengeance was what he really wanted. Joseph knew that his brothers deserved to be punished. Yet, at the same time, something inside him cried out for reconciliation with them. It was a feeling he could not ignore.

Joseph chose forgiveness, no longer feeling the necessity to punish his brothers. He was free to make peace with them. Their moment of reconciliation is described with simple eloquence in the Book of Genesis. It reads there, "And Joseph said to his brothers, 'I am Joseph. Does my father yet live?' " The brothers could not believe their ears and so once again, Joseph spoke to them and said, "Come near to me, I pray you. I am Joseph, your brother, whom you sold into Egypt."

Joseph had been betrayed. He had been hated by his brothers. But he had reached a moment—a transforming moment—when he could put down the memory of the wrong they had done. It was impossible to carry it any longer. Filled with emotion, Joseph cried and he forgave his brothers. This story tells us that even though reconciliation is difficult to achieve, forgiveness can triumph nonetheless.

TEARS OF ESTRANGEMENT

Only infrequently am I fortunate enough to see the tears of reconciliation. Far more often, I have come to know the tears of people we all know. They are the tears of some who will pick up this book because there is a void in their lives too painful to be dismissed. And they are the tears of the powerful and famous who have the world at their fingertips, but live with an emptiness in the heart. Have we not all watched interviews of people blessed with so much in life? And yet, in moments of candor, as the discussion focuses on their family life, you hear their voices crack and you see their eyes well up with tears as they speak of the estrangement from a loved one.

I cannot forget watching a televised interview with Nancy Reagan. The former first lady spoke confidently on a wide range of issues. But when the subject turned to her family life, her eyes began to tear. Questioned about the well-publicized estrangement from her daughter Patti, Mrs. Reagan could barely speak. This woman had virtually everything that anyone could desire. In the years she spent in the White House, she had accumulated enormous power. What she didn't have was the love of her daughter. Her tears told of a void that power and fame could not fill.

In Jerusalem, there is an ancient wall. We call it the Western Wall. For the Jewish people, it is a sacred site. Many years ago, people began leaving notes to God in the cracks and crevices of that 2,000-year-old wall. Over the centuries, these notes have been pressed into the wall with the hope that a special prayer will be answered. Some have written asking for the recovery of a loved one. Others have prayed for peace. There have been those who asked for special strength, as well as those who look to God for help in resolving a family conflict.

Each time I make a pilgrimage to Israel, congregants ask me to take along their prayers and insert them into the wall. On my last trip to Israel, a member of my congregation approached me and said, "Rabbi, this is so important to me. Please make certain to put this prayer into the wall. It is a simple prayer. I want you to know what I am asking of God." He opened the paper and read to me these words: "Dear God, You have given me so much in life. You have blessed me with health and with wealth. Please help my son to find a way to forgive me. I love him and I want him back. I miss him and I want him close again." The light in this father's life had been dimmed. For years, he had not known true joy or happiness. Still, he lived with the hope that his prayer would be answered and that forgiveness would come from a son with whom he longed to be reconciled.

RECONCILIATION DAY

The emotional thread that binds so many of us together is the pain of living with a broken relationship and the never-dying hope that perhaps, a new beginning is still possible. It was this amalgam of emotions which prompted one woman to write this moving letter to Ann Landers. She wrote, "I've suddenly become aware that the years are flying by. Time somehow seems more precious. My parents suddenly seem old. My aunts and uncles are sick. I haven't seen some of my cousins for several years. Then my thoughts turn to the dark side. I remember the feelings I've hurt and I recall my own hurt feelings—the misunderstandings and the unmended fences that separated us and set up barriers.

"I think of my mother and her sister who haven't spoken to each other in five years. As a result of their argument, my cousin and I haven't spoken either. What a waste of precious time! I'm sure that there are millions of people in your reading audience who could tell similar stories.

"Wouldn't it be terrific if a special day would be set aside to reach out and make amends? We would call it 'Reconciliation Day.' Everyone would vow to write a letter or make a phone call—and mend a strained or broken relationship. It would also be the day on which we would all agree to accept the olive branch extended by a former friend. This day could be the starting point. We could go on from here to heal the wounds in our hearts and rejoice in a brand new beginning."

I'm certain that this woman's story sounds hauntingly familiar to so many people. Like this woman, we tend to let the years pass by because reaching out to someone who has been lost from our lives is one of the most difficult things we can do. But time is precious and life is too short to permit misunderstandings and quarrels to run on year after year. No one need wait for a "Reconciliation Day" to do what could be done today. For any one of us, "Reconciliation Day" can come right now—and joy and gladness can once again be our tomorrow.

CHAPTER 2

The Many Faces of the Hardened Heart

"One who has begged for forgiveness should not be so cruel as not to forgive."

—Rashi

There is a story I tell of two friends who traveled together as they went from town to town. While traveling, one of them fell into a river, and the other leaped in and saved him from drowning. The friend who had almost drowned had his servants carve these words on the large rock nearby: "Traveler! In this place, Nagib risked his life and saved the life of his friend Mussa."

The friends then resumed their journey—only to find themselves, on the return trip, at the very spot where one had saved the life of the other. As they sat and spoke, a difference of opinion turned into a quarrel. Words were exchanged and the one who had almost drowned was hit in the face by his friend. He picked himself up, took a stick, and wrote these words in the sand: "Traveler! In this place, Nagib, in a trivial argument, broke the heart of his friend Mussa."

Mussa was asked by one of his men why he would carve

the story of his friend's heroism in stone, but tell the story of his cruelty only in the sand. He responded, "I will always cherish the memory of how my friend Nagib saved me in a time of danger. But the grave injury he just gave me—it is my hope that I will forgive him for it, even before the words fade from the sand."

This memorable story tells that, in a world in which forgiveness is not considered a basic tool of survival, there is something fundamentally right about one's commitment to another, moving that person to choose forgiveness over anger. Countless hours of urging people to forgive has led me to understand that for some, the prospect of reconciliation is strong enough to overcome their anger and hurt. For other people, it's the most difficult thing to do. Counseling them to forgive is like coming up against a stone wall.

It is at times such as these that I recall the story of a captive who was brought before King James II of England. The king taunted the prisoner, saying "You know that it is in my power to pardon you?" The scared, shaking prisoner replied, "Yes, I know it is in your power to pardon me, but it is not in your nature." The prisoner felt that it might not be human nature to forgive.

The work I've done with people seems to confirm the prisoner's observation. I recall counseling a young man who wanted nothing more than reconciliation with his father. They had a history of hurting and disappointing each other. I was asked by this young man to contact his father to arrange a meeting. The father responded to me in a letter which read as follows: "I thank you for your interest. I hope you understand that I can never forgive my son for what he has done. He turned against me. I've come to accept that I have one less son. For me, forgiveness is out of the question."

13

I had hoped that my invitation would arouse within the father a desire to meet with his son. I did not expect his cold and cavalier rejection. His letter showed nothing of the emotional pain we would expect from someone who had cast aside his relationship with a child.

At times, it seems—to use a popular biblical metaphor—that the hearts of so many people we know have become hardened. All too often, I've heard moving pleas for forgiveness that failed to pierce the hearts of those to whom they were directed. Just as often, I've reached out on behalf of people who wanted forgiveness—only to have my own efforts rebuffed. Yet surprisingly, and shockingly, there are people who feel little pain or remorse as they write family members and friends out of their lives. People have become too hard and too tough. And though these qualities may be considered by many to be useful outside the home, they are not the foundation stones upon which reconciliation can flourish.

One of the most studied collections of Jewish literature is the interpretation of the Bible called the Midrash. A legend of the Midrash underscores that our world—and all human relations—cannot survive unless there is compassion. This legend tells us that when God set out to create the world, He realized that were He to judge people by the strictest standards of justice, nobody would survive. In like manner, God understood that if mercy alone became the judgment, people would transgress at will, assured of their eventual acquittal. So God created both attributes. People would be judged by a code of justice which would be tempered with compassion. In this way, sensitivity and mercy became part of the structure of the cosmos.

It is not surprising, therefore, that throughout Jewish literature, God is lovingly portrayed as both the "judge of all the earth'' and also the One who is merciful and forgiving. The teachers of Judaism speak of a God who is ever willing to accept those who reach out to Him in the hope of finding a compassionate, caring, and loving response.

There are times when I search in vain to find in human beings some of the compassion associated with their Creator. Believing that they are just and that their indignation is right-eous, some simply refuse to forgive. Where mercy and compassion are most needed, they are at times most lacking. Reconciliation comes from the heart of a person who knows that righteousness can lead to self-righteousness and hard-heartedness to the destruction of human relations.

It is not accidental that the sages of my tradition thought that a heart of goodness is the only antidote to the harshness and cruelty of life. A story in the Talmud tells of one rabbi who sent his students out to observe the world. He wanted them to leave the study hall and take note of the qualities of character which were most praiseworthy among people. When the students returned to the academy, they shared the results of what they had observed. The rabbi was most pleased with the student who said possessing a good heart is the most praiseworthy trait of character.

What is a good heart? It is a heart that can feel the anguish of another who desires to be forgiven. A good heart is one that is compassionate enough to respond with love and tenderness, even when the dictates of justice might suggest otherwise. When we look for a humane response from another person, we plead, "Have a heart." We look to the heart, hoping that a person will be moved enough to overlook a wrong, and be compassionate enough to feel another's anguish.

When I began collecting the stories and personal accounts included in this book, I came across an article about a support group for parents separated from their children. I was able to speak with a member of this group who had long mourned the estrangement which separated her from her son. Over the years, she had struggled in vain to reach out to her son. Time after time, he had refused to answer her calls or respond to her letters. Could there be any hurt more devastating than that of a parent who is left to mourn the living death of a relationship with a child?

As we spoke of the book I was preparing, the woman said, "If only your book will help children, and all people, to understand how painful it is to live like this. Maybe someone will read it and be moved enough to forgive. Maybe a child will come to understand the dreadful hurt a parent feels when he or she is rejected. And maybe that son or daughter will be touched and respond with a little bit of compassion." This parent, like many people, lives with the hope that one day, forgiveness will come from a loved one whose heart will no longer be so hard and unfeeling.

Religious leaders of every faith have had the experience of meeting with a family prior to a funeral and being told not to mention the name of one or more family members during the course of the eulogy. Angrily, those gathered relate the story of a wrong done years ago and still considered unforgivable. It is not uncommon today for people to be told that they are not welcome at a funeral and that they will be barred from entering the chapel. There was a time I thought that death had the capacity to soften hearts and bring people together. Though it occasionally does happen, far more often, it leaves people harder and even more unreachable. At times, I'm left praying that family members will just be civil to one another. If, at the time of death, there can't be love, at least let there not be war.

Throughout my career in the rabbinate, I have been involved in hospital chaplaincy. My work has made me a believer in the connection which exists between a patient's emotional well-being and longed-for physical healing. A patient needs to feel the support of loved ones and the concern of friends and members of the community.

One of the most difficult conversations I have is with people who are struggling to recover their health as they deal with emotional pain. This pain comes from knowing that a family member refuses to be with them, even in their hour of need. A patient will ask, "What did I do so wrong that my own child won't come to see me when I'm so ill? How can my child be so unfeeling?" The same questions are asked about other family members whose absence is similarly felt.

Once, while making my rounds in our community hospital, I met a man who told me of a conversation he had with his father just prior to his father's death. He said, "My father died too painfully. There was no peace. For years, he had been trying to reach out to my brother. Even as he was dying, my brother wouldn't budge. My father kept wondering if there was something about the way he lived that had served as a model to make my brother cold and unfeeling. He died questioning himself and the life that he lived.

"It's funny, my father knew what I thought of my brother's actions. And before he died, he said, 'I have one request, should your brother ever turn to you—forgive him for what he's done to me. I don't want to go knowing that you will not forgive him.' I'll never understand what made my brother so unfeeling. Why did he have to be so uncaring? Why couldn't my father go in peace?" His father could not go in peace because he had a son who lived with a heart that had hardened, a heart which was unwilling to respond to the cries for peace from a father who was dying.

LIVING IN A THROWAWAY AGE

What is becoming frighteningly obvious is that some people believe that relationships are expendable and people are disposable. Living in a throwaway age, we have become accustomed to getting rid of that which is no longer functioning properly. We believe it's simpler and more convenient to replace than it is to repair. That philosophy may work well with coffee makers or toasters, but in real life, it destroys the way in which people relate to one another. Frequently, when I try to move someone to forgiveness, the response I hear is, "I don't need him anymore." I'm asked, "Why should I care? I can easily make a new life for myself without her." Forgiveness can be elusive in a world in which so many believe that no one is irreplaceable.

Recently, I read a full-page advertisement for a personal robot. The ad copy was impressive. Citing the capabilities of this robot, the ad read, "It walks, talks, and will wait on you hand and foot. It is just like a member of the family." The advertisement tells us a lot about what family means in contemporary society. It suggests that membership in a family is based on what you can give and the service that you can render. The ad ought to serve as a warning to us all. For when membership in a family is based on the ability to serve, then those who disappoint us, or fail to serve us well, become expendable.

Not long ago, I was told about a rabbi who, while conducting a wedding ceremony, shared some personal insights with the bride and groom. The rabbi taught that the words "untie" and "unite" have the same letters. Only the placement of the letter "I" in each word leads to two very different meanings. He went on to teach that in marriage, or any other relationship, where we put the "I" is crucial. When one person's focus is on "what I get" or "what's in it for me," a relationship can flounder. However, when people truly unite, when "I" gives way to "we," and when family members and friends are cherished for what they are and not what they can do, something enduring has been brought into being.

I know of families in which every member routinely disappoints and hurts one another. They always seem to fall short of each other's expectations. Nonetheless, there is, above all, a commitment to family and to each other that binds them together. They know that there is something irreplacably precious which overshadows the wounds and bruised feelings. Each relationship survives because those involved understand that even a flawed relationship is not to be casually discarded. Families such as these remind us that true family is found where people share a sense of history, a dream of a common future, and a rootedness in the lives of one another.

In recent years, the telephone company has reminded us in its advertisements that "We're all connected." In one of its commercials, a young man is seen walking out on either his wife or girlfriend after a disagreement. He angrily slams the door and at that moment, the only thing that matters to him are his feelings and his needs. But as he walks around the city, he notices others walking hand in hand. It is then that he realizes that life means being connected to people that you love, even when they disappoint you. Understanding this, he steps into a phone booth and calls his young lady to say, "I'm sorry.'' At that point, we hear the familiar theme song reminding us that we're all connected. Along with promoting the role of the telephone at important times in our lives, this commercial also is wisely telling us that when we understand that we're connected, in spite of the inevitable hurts and betrayals, we open the door to forgiveness.

A MATTER OF PRIDE

Several years ago, I offered my own version of a guaranteed weight-loss program. Unlike other highly touted diet plans, mine did not require giving up any of the foods people love to eat. I simply suggested that if people were to lay aside a grudge or forgive someone, they would feel as though they were ten pounds lighter.

Some time later, a member of my congregation called and said, ''My brother and I had an argument several months ago. I've been waiting for him to be the one who called to apologize. I wasn't going to make the first move. Then, I remembered something you said and I realized how foolish I was to allow my pride to prevent me from reaching out to him. Suddenly, it made sense to get rid of the animosity which was weighing me down.''

It often seems that pride, which has the capacity to carry us to our greatest achievements, is the very same emotion that erects some of the most formidable barriers to forgiveness. Pride is the enemy of forgiveness. We all know someone who misses out on so much in life because of an unwillingness to be the first one to make a move.

One of the most important biblical figures was Aaron the

brother of Moses. Tradition describes Aaron as a pursuer of peace. He personally took upon himself the task of restoring peaceful relations among people. Aaron understood how pride could stand in the way of reconciliation.

When Aaron discovered two people had been quarreling he visited privately with each of them. He would go to the first person and say, "I know that your friend is sorry for all that has happened. He desperately wants there to be a reconciliation between the two of you." Then, Aaron would go to the other party involved in the dispute and say, "I know that your friend is sorry for what he did. He wants to be forgiven." When the two people met, personal pride was no longer an issue. Each believed that the other had made the first move. Aaron successfully eliminated pride as an obstacle to peace. As a "lover of peace and pursuer of peace," Aaron knew that there are times when peace can only be possible after pride ceases to be an issue.

Parents will often ask me, "Why should I be the one who takes the first step? Isn't it up to my child to say something first? Doesn't being a parent count for anything any more?" I generally respond by saying that love is too precious to be lost because of protocol. The prophet Malachi understood this when he said that one day, the prophet Elijah would "turn the hearts of parents to the children and the hearts of children to the parents." Although Malachi knew of the respect and reverence due a parent, he believed that the urgent task of healing requires that a parent's pride or the honor due a parent's position in the family must, at times, yield for the sake of peace.

The prophet's instructions to parents go to the heart of the matter. His words are a reminder that pride must never prevent any of us from making the first gesture toward reconciliation. My tradition teaches that when people quarrel, the one who yields first is the greater of the two. When speaking with people who are facing the end of their life, rarely do I find them proud because they stubbornly stood on principle and refused to make a gesture which might have led to forgiveness. Far more common are the lamentations of those who understand at that time, better than ever before, that they sacrificed too much for the sake of their pride.

One of my favorite movies is *On Golden Pond.* In part, the movie portrays the relationship of a grown daughter named Chelsea and her father Norman, who had been walking delicately on the fault line of an unsatisfactory relationship. Each time they were together, there was uneasiness and awkwardness. They moved cautiously around each other, trying to disguise the fact that they wanted more from one another and their relationship. But, both Chelsea and Norman were too proud to ask for more.

At one point, Chelsea, filled with rage, confronted her mother. She was angry because she couldn't remember ever knowing the love of her father. Her mother responded by reminding her that her father was old and infirm—and that little time remained for them to find each other. Understanding that it was up to her to take the first step, Chelsea finally approached her father and asked for the opportunity to renew their relationship. She told him that it seemed they were forever angry with each other and that the time had come for them to exchange that anger for friendship.

Life, as we know so well, does not always imitate art. There are people who adamantly refuse to be the one to initiate the dialogue. Life teaches us, however, that there is too much to be lost to permit pride to block our path to forgiveness.

I once counseled a woman in her sixties who had always been disappointed in her relationship with her elderly father. She only knew her father as aloof and disinterested. This woman had permitted years to pass waiting for him to change. As time went by, their relationship didn't improve. He grew old, weak, and increasingly dependent upon her assistance.

The woman came to see me because her pride was making it difficult for her to help this man who gave her so little over the course of a lifetime. I worked with her on using whatever time was left to make peace with her father. I remember commenting, "You waited your whole life, hoping that he would approach you. Don't wait any longer believing it to be his responsibility to make the first move. Use whatever time the two of you have together to set this relationship right."

This woman spent the last two years caring for her father and, at long last, getting to know him. In those two years, she found something precious. When the time came for his funeral, she was content knowing that for a brief time, they had shared what she had always wanted. The woman came to appreciate that it's just not important who takes the first step toward reconciliation. The only thing which is important is that someone decides to take responsibility for a relationship and resolves to do what is possible to restore it.

SHIFTING THE BLAME

One of the most imposing obstacles to reconciliation is the tendency people have to shift the blame onto others. Placing the blame on someone else is as old as Adam, who claimed that it was Eve who had urged him to eat the forbidden fruit. Adam's step away from responsibility is not at all shocking to many in our own generation, who have grown comfortable with the philosophy: "Don't blame me."

There are many people who simply refuse to accept responsibility for their actions and for the hurt their actions have caused. They prefer instead to blame someone else, for that renders them pure and unaccountable; they remain blameless and beyond any moral condemnation.

In life, choices often come down to accepting the blame for something which has gone wrong in a relationship or refusing to acknowledge responsibility. Only when we realize to what extent the "don't blame me" syndrome diminishes our ability to act responsibly in a relationship can we move to reconciliation. A person I know well told me of a tear in his relationship with his brother. He said, "For one year, my brother and I didn't speak. I blamed him and he blamed me for what had happened. Neither of us was willing to accept responsibility. We had been so close. But then, we walked out of each other's lives. That year was a living hell for the two of us. Thankfully, our wives decided that enough time had passed and they arranged a surprise encounter. When we saw each other, I understood how foolish we had been. Because neither of us wanted to accept the blame for the misunderstanding which had occurred, we lived for one year without each other."

There are people who will go to great lengths in order to be absolved of any link to a wrongdoing or a moral failing. And yet, we know instinctively that a relationship requires one person being courageous enough to reject the "don't blame me" syndrome and accept responsibility for what has gone wrong. Where love is strong, blame becomes very insignificant.

THE FEAR OF BEING HURT AGAIN

Frequently, the people I counsel begin by making clear their feeling that there is futility in forgiving. They cite all the past episodes of hurt. They feel justifiably reluctant about forgiving out of a fear of being hurt again. They sum it up by saying, "I've tried many times already; nothing is ever going to change." In relationships marked by chronic, long-term disappointment, it is understandably difficult for people to believe that forgiveness and reconciliation could be long lasting.

A father once pleaded with me to do whatever was necessary to set up a counseling session with his son. I contacted the son, who was absolutely resolute in his belief that any effort would be futile and unproductive. I persisted, and he did join his father for a counseling session. The father was contrite, acknowledging the things he had done to upset his son in the past. The son was unmoved. When I phoned him the next day, he was unwilling to go beyond that first meeting. I indicated to him that I thought we had made substantial progress in our session together. He remarked, "I've been down this road before—it leads nowhere."

After our conversation, I knew what I wanted to say but had not. I wanted to tell this man's son that there is no place for arithmetic—for counting the number of times we have forgiven when a precious relationship is at stake. And I wanted to tell him that to believe that what has happened in the past

25

must necessarily be repeated in the future is to dismiss the possibility that a human being can change.

At the heart of the forgiving response is the thought that people can change, grow, and overcome their past. Unfortunately, the son never permitted himself to believe that his father could be any different in the future than he had been in the past that they shared together. To this day, his father's eyes well up with tears every time he mentions his son and thinks about the reconciliation that never was.

My religious tradition tells of a God that does not write people off. Patiently, He waits for people, not counting the number of times they have failed Him in the past. With love He waits, believing that people can transcend themselves and that their tomorrow can be different from their yesterday.

This philosophy is found in the story of a man who was preparing for the approach of the High Holy Days. An acquaintance, who was also something of a skeptic, asked why he was going to go through the routine of repenting for all his sins if, year after year, he only commits them all over again. The man replied, saying, "You're right. From year to year, I repent and succumb to many of the same sins for which I've repented. But each year, I believe that maybe this will be the year that I will change."

Love looks forward—it looks to the promise of tomorrow. Those who love look forward, believing that a relationship can be transformed and improved. Enduring love looks beyond pride and blame, and it seeks forgiveness.

CHAPTER 3

Anger Is Too Heavy to Carry

"Forgive and forget if you can, but forgive anyway."
—Henry Van Dyke

Whenever I'm invited to speak about forgiveness and reconciliation, a group of people usually remain after my talk to ask personal questions. One of the questions most frequently asked is, "How can I forget what was done to me?" For them, forgetting is the biggest obstacle to forgiveness. However, forgiving does not demand that we simultaneously perform the more difficult task of forgetting.

Few of us ever can fully forget the wrongs which have been done to us. Acts of betrayal are not easily erased from our minds. Were forgiveness to wait for forgetfulness, reconciliation could rarely occur. Amnesia is not a prelude to forgiveness. Forgiveness is knowing that something happened which made us curious and then deciding, in spite of everything, to deny anger its power.

Those who decide to forgive do so for many reasons. Some come to the realization that they are unwilling to sacrifice a cherished relationship. Others forgive because they no longer want to revisit the betrayals of the past. They look for a way to let go of the hurts, bind up their wounds, and move on. They have come to recognize that feelings have the capacity, as Louis B. Smedes has written, to "hurt the hater more than the hated." Make no mistake about it—anger and the misery it creates can become a curse in the life of a human being. Reconciliation becomes a possibility when a person realizes the emotional cost of being stuck in a painful past.

Some important ideas on this subject were offered in an article which appeared in the *New York Times*. Researchers studied the emotional health of men who had reached the age of 65. They found that one of the most constant predictors of well being at that age was "the ability to handle emotional crises maturely."

Having followed over 150 men since they graduated college in the early 1940s, the researchers learned that handling life's blows without becoming bitter and living without collecting injustices contributed significantly to the emotional well being of the men who were studied. What is apparent from their research is that people who live their lives warehousing the wrongs done to them suffer emotional scars which affect their long-term ability to find happiness, contentment, and satisfaction in life.

Years ago, I enjoyed reading Herman Melville's *Moby Dick*. On one level, it is an exciting adventure story read generation after generation. On a deeper level, it is a story about what anger can do to the person who surrenders to its power.

Early in the novel, Moby Dick, the great white whale, bites off the leg of Captain Ahab. Ahab is consumed by his anger and his need for vengeance. Filled with rage, he devotes his life to tracking down Moby Dick. As the story comes to its end, Ahab has his encounter with Moby Dick. All that remains is to harpoon the great whale and taste the sweetness of revenge. But as Ahab throws the harpoon into the whale, he becomes ensnarled in the rope. Ahab is pulled into the sea and drowns. Perhaps this timeless story is teaching us that it is important to put down the hurts and the desire to avenge those who wounded us lest we end up destroying our lives.

Many years before Melville's classic was written, an anecdote was told about the life of one of Judaism's sages, Mar Zutra. By the example of his life, he taught his students a valuable lesson. Mar Zutra followed the custom of saying, each night before he retired, "I forgive all who hurt me today." He understood the imperfections of humanity. He forgave wholeheartedly those who disappointed him. For Mar Zutra, forgiveness was a gift that he gave freely to others, as well as himself.

This wise sage appreciated that he would sleep better and live happier having removed all the bitterness and hatred from his heart. Mar Zutra knew that those who torment themselves by harboring grudges and by reprising outdated feuds pay a heavy price for their refusal to outgrow bitterness and vindictiveness. Knowing this, he chose forgiveness each and every night. In doing so, he chose life.

In the Book of Leviticus, there is a verse which simply says, "You shall not hate your fellow in your heart." As I study that verse from year to year, I think of all the people I've known who have permitted anger and hatred to smolder and consume them. If you've ever carried anger, you know how truly wise this biblical advice is. A contemporary rabbi, Rabbi Samuel Stahl, has written that when anger metastasizes within, it becomes "a psychic carcinoma." The words of Leviticus are telling. Don't permit the anger you feel to find a dwelling place in your heart. Don't permit its appetite for vengeance to become firmly fixed in your soul. For over time, it will become a burden too heavy to carry.

One of my favorite books of the Bible is the Book of Proverbs. Throughout the generations and today, it continues to teach us significant lessons. In chapter 27, we are offered this insight: "A stone is heavy and sand is weighty, but anger heavier than them both." Anger can be the heaviest burden we carry. It is weighty baggage which has the capacity to anchor us to the past, causing us to forsake the joys of the present. It is the one burden we can put down and should put down, if not for the sake of those who hurt us, then certainly for our own well being.

Some time ago, I met a woman in the hospital who had requested a visit by the hospital chaplain. She had been hospitalized for tests and observation. Several days had passed and the doctors were still perplexed. Although medically she appeared to be fine, she continued to complain about her condition.

As we spoke, I asked the woman if there was something happening in her life which was contributing to her being particularly anxious. She told me that in several weeks, she was going to attend the wedding of a relative. Though it was still weeks off, she was anticipating seeing her sister from whom she had been long separated. Years ago, they had fought over the provision of care for an elderly parent. She accused her sister of shirking her responsibilities. There were ugly accusations made on both sides and the two of them walked out of each other's lives.

From that time, the anger that the woman felt for her sister dominated her life. She dreaded every family occasion which brought the two of them together. I asked her what she wanted to do about it. Her reply was surprising. "Believe it or not," she said, "I want to stop being angry with my sister. I'm tired of it. Once we were close and I would like to have that back again." I remarked to her, "When every time of joy becomes a bitter experience, you've already waited too long to forgive. Your sister is just a phone call away."

When I returned several days later, the woman was preparing to leave the hospital. Something about her had changed. The heaviness of her expression had gone and was replaced with a smile. She had called her sister and they had begun to patch things up. For the first time in years, she was looking forward to being with her sister. No longer did she have to suffer the physical and emotional anxiety which came in anticipation of every one of their encounters. That was not the first, nor was it the last time I have met a person who suffered physically from anger left unresolved.

Recently, I read the story of a young woman who grew up in a home in which her father physically abused her and her mother. Her father beat them and blamed them for all the problems he was experiencing. This young woman suffered for years from incapacitating headaches. After years of treatment, she was finally convinced that it was not medication, but reconciliation with her father that was needed.

Long after the beatings and verbal assaults had ended, the young woman was still angry with her father. It was this anger which was limiting her ability to live fully with her husband and her children. Summoning her courage, she drove to her parents' apartment. She sat down with her mother and her father and they spoke of their shared past. She then approached her father and said, "Daddy, I forgive you for everything that happened when I was a child. I love you." More than tears were shed that day. According to this young woman,

31

she was also able to shed the headaches which had plagued her for so long.

A number of years ago, a popular television talk show devoted a program to the subject of making peace with one's parents. On the panel were a psychologist and several parents and children. During the program, Lisa and her father, Jay, told their story of estrangement. Lisa was born shortly after her parents were married. At the time, they were less than excited about what should have been a blessed event in their lives.

Lisa was an unwanted intrusion into her father's life. As she grew up, she felt the pain of never having been fully accepted by her father. Lisa spoke of how she lived her entire life feeling insecure and left out. The relationship she had with her father affected her emotional well being in every conceivable way. She carried that sense of rejection and all the emotional torment which came along with it until she could bear it no longer.

Lisa contacted her father and together, they met with a psychologist. He suggested that only by letting go of the anger and resentment would they be able to significantly connect with each other. They could give themselves the chance to feel the love between them. Here was the opportunity to change the course of their relationship for the rest of their lives.

Rabbi Joshua, having observed human relations, taught that "hatred puts a person out of the world." I believe he meant that anger which seeks no reconciliation cuts a person off from real living. Those who reject any resolution of a personal conflict impose a life sentence on themselves. Most of us have known people who have severed ties with a family member or friend. Try as they may to go on with life, it never is quite the same. Their efforts to even the score often leave them alone, miserable, and cut off from the world and the people who are important to them.

JOSEPH REVISITED

Let's return to Joseph and his brothers to see how a moment of transformation occurs—a transformation that lets go of the past and opens up the door to a new beginning. The Joseph we meet in the Bible had good reason to be vindictive. His brothers had committed a treacherous act. Yet, having lived for years cut off from his brothers and his entire family, Joseph chose instead to forgive.

The narrative of the Bible enables us to accompany Joseph as he journeys from anger to forgiveness. As we know, Joseph saw his brothers for the first time since they had thrown him into the pit when they arrived in Egypt to purchase food. The brothers were brought before Joseph, who was second in command in Egypt. The power of his position gave him the ability to punish his brothers had he wished to do so. It appears that he plotted and considered it.

Joseph sensed the distress he was causing his brothers, but he came to realize that this was not what he wanted to accomplish. Momentarily, he had tasted vengeance, but it was too bitter. He learned that his wounds could not be healed by hurting them. All he felt at that instant was that for years, he had lived apart from his brothers and he no longer wanted to live that way. Surrounded by servants and palace officials, he was still lonely for family. Hoping that reconciliation would relieve his own emotional pain, Joseph chose to forgive. He was ready to once again be part of the world into which he was born and which he had sorely missed.

SHADOWS OF ANGER

There are people who never experience this moment of transformation. They conspicuously parade their feelings, believing that in doing so, they are punishing those who wronged them. They attempt to get even by being visibly miserable and beyond consolation. They choose to live in the shadows, not because they have to, but because it is their way of getting revenge. Those who follow this path discover that it offers no real consolation.

From the life of Elizabeth Kenny, the nurse who developed a treatment for polio, we learn a wonderful lesson. She was asked how she managed to maintain such a cheerful countenance. The person speaking with her said, "I suppose you were just born calm and smiling." Elizabeth Kenny laughed and said, "Oh no, as a girl I often lost my temper. But one day when I became angry at a friend over some trivial matter, my mother said to me: 'Elizabeth, anyone who angers you, conquers you.' And I have never forgotten her words." If only people understood how much power they yield to those who have caused them to feel anger and hatred. They permit another person to rob them of something as precious as their sense of well being and personal happiness.

One evening, I spoke with a congregant in my study. For many years, this man had been a regular Sabbath worshipper. Suddenly, he disappeared from view. Although he had retained his membership in our congregation, I noticed his absence each and every Sabbath. He shared with me the story of why he had stopped coming to synagogue.

This man had an argument with another member of our congregation. Determined to show everyone how angry he was, he stopped coming to services and thereby gave up something that had become an important part of his life. In his anger, he had given another person control over his life. He had come to deny himself a source of personal satisfaction that had meant so much to him. If his life was less than it once was, then anger was the cause.

Anger has the capacity to intrude into every aspect of our lives. Jay Feldman, a writer now living in California, in an article entitled "A Time to Forgive, But Never Forget," wrote of the seething anger he had long felt for Walter O'Malley, the late owner of the Dodgers. Feldman had hated O'Malley since he moved the Brooklyn Dodgers to Los Angeles in 1958. Feldman told that the heartbreak caused by O'Malley's betrayal made him turn away from baseball for nearly 20 years. Some might consider that to be an exaggerated response, but the scars caused by the departure of the Dodgers from Brooklyn have never healed.

And so, Feldman carried around a hatred for O'Malley and a disillusionment for the game which, at the tender age of 14, he learned revolved around money. As a result of his feelings for O'Malley, he cut himself off from the game of baseball.

But Feldman experienced a special moment. He wrote, "I was stopped short by a brief note in the newspaper commemorating the tenth anniversary of Walter O'Malley's death. Unexpectedly, an involuntary thought formed in my mind: I'm carrying around a grudge against a guy who's been dead for ten years! The recognition of the absurdity of that was the first

35

crack in the structure as I began to consider whether I really wanted to go on hating a memory." Feldman decided to forgive the one man he hated more than anyone else. Coming to the realization that "times change, conditions change, people change—it's time to move on," Feldman finally forgave Walter O'Malley.

In one of the most surprising statements in Jewish literature, we're told that God has his own special prayers. They are simple prayers, which tell us where God feels most vulnerable. One of God's prayers is, "May it be My will that My compassion conquer My anger." Above all, God desires reconciliation with the people He has created and so He prays for the compassion necessary to overcome His anger. God understands the enormous negative power of anger and so He prays to be rid of it. His vulnerability is a mirror image of our own.

Look around—it's easy to see that anger brings destruction into the world. Shattered relationships have become commonplace. Perhaps, then, God's prayer should be ours as well. Let our compassion be strong enough to subdue our anger.

CHAPTER 4

Finding Our Way Back to Each Other

"Every man should keep a fair-sized cemetery in which to bury the faults of his friend."

—Henry Ward Beecher

There is an old legend told of two monks who came to a muddy road. As they were preparing to cross to the other side of the road, a beautiful girl approached. Seeing that she was terribly upset that she would have to walk through mud, one of the monks picked her up and carried her to the other side. His companion was absolutely amazed at the sight but could not bring himself to say anything. He remained silent and disappointed as he watched his friend abandon the discipline of their order.

When they arrived at the lodging where they would spend the night, the second monk confronted his friend. "Monks must have nothing to do with women," he said angrily. "It is too dangerous. We must stay away from them, and we certainly must never touch a woman." The first monk turned and asked, "Are you still carrying that young girl? I put her down at the other side of the road, but you have carried her all this way.''

As I've counseled and observed, I have tried to understand what it is that enables some people to put down anger and let go of animosity while others insist on carrying it wherever they go. Early on, I realized that the art of giving is at the heart of forgiving. Many people I've counseled believe that they are justified in withholding forgiveness. Those who received little, who were abandoned by parents, spurned by children, or disappointed by a spouse can easily rationalize carrying their hurts forever. A common refrain in the early stages of reconciliation counseling is the question, ''How can anyone expect me to forgive after what was done to me?''

When reconciliation counseling is successful, it enables people to see life as more than an equation in which the giving and getting must be equal. Forgiveness is offered not because it is owed to another person. We give it as we come to understand that life is made meaningful by what we have given and not by what we have gained.

REMEMBERING WHEN

Knowing that there have been times when we were forgiven for our faults and imperfections should enable us to be more forgiving of others. Once we look carefully at our own lives, we realize that there have been occasions where the people we disappointed responded with understanding and love. When we remember those times and how good it felt to be forgiven, we can be moved to extend the gift of forgiveness to others.

I recall the reflections of a woman who said to me, "For a long time, too long a time, I had permitted a feud to go on between my son and me. I thought the only way I could get back at my son was to let him feel my hostility. As far as I was concerned, the longer I denied him forgiveness, the better. Then I realized that I was withholding from my son what I had received from others in the past. What came to mind was a time when I let my sister down even though she needed me very much. Believe me, I felt terrible about it. Thankfully, my sister's anger didn't last long. Recalling how I felt when she said she forgave me, I understood that I couldn't deny my son the same gift of love."

THE GLORY OF LOVE

Each day when we leave our homes, we enter a world in which people bruise us all the time. We are supposed to be rugged individuals capable of bearing up in a competitive world filled with mean streets and tough people. Threatened by the outside world, we look toward loved ones with ever greater expectations and needs. We want and desperately need the people close to us to be different from everyone else. We want them to be people we can trust. And in turn, they look to us, hoping that we will not betray them.

Sadly, and perhaps inevitably, we all disappoint those we love. We all fall short and we all bring some pain into the lives of loved ones. There are two responses when someone we love has hurt us. Some will hold tight to their anger, magnifying the hurt done to them. Others, whose love is mature and understanding, will respond by offering reconciliation because they find no delight in revenge or retaliation.

Do you recall the old musical standard, "The Glory of Love?" The simple lyrics teach a valuable lesson about forgiveness. It's hard to forget the words, "You've got to give a little, take a little, let your heart break a little. That's the story of, that's the glory of love." The lyrics are telling us that when people love, there will be times of heartache and hurt—that sometimes, the people from whom we expect so much will let us down. There will be moments when, in return for love, our hearts will be broken. The glory of love is that we can look at the shortcomings, the mistakes, and the faults as insignificant and focus instead on the commitments which unite us.

The Wizard of Oz made his wisest observation some 50 years ago when he told his visitors that hearts will not be practical until they are unbreakable. In every relationship of love, there will be heartbreak. But when love looks forward, we see through our hurt and permit our hearts to mend. We open ourselves anew and reconnect to those people we care about.

The author of Proverbs offered similar advice when he taught, "Hatred stirs up strife—but love covers all transgressions." I don't think it was the intention of this wise teacher to suggest that we overlook or ignore what has been hurtful to us. When we are betrayed by someone close, the transgression shouldn't be passed over. However, this teaching does suggest that love should enable us to put our hurts and disappointments into perspective.

Several years ago, I received a call from a woman who asked me to meet with her family. She was obviously under great stress. Her husband and daughter had been estranged for well over a year. The daughter had at last agreed to enter into family counseling.

I listened to both the daughter and the father as they spoke of their relationship. Their life together was one of unrealized expectations. Neither could easily recall when they last felt good about each other. At times, it was difficult listening as he father spoke of his sense of failure. He understood that he had not been the father his daughter wanted. And as it angered her, it tormented him.

During one of our sessions, he said to his daughter, ''I remember doing so many wonderful things with you when you were younger. But somehow, all I can recall from these past few years is you being mad at me. I wish I could tell you how much you mean to me, how much I love you. I wish I could make up what was lost. All I can ask of you is that you forgive me for not being the father I wanted to be and was not.''

After all the words had been spoken, the father turned to his daughter and asked that she love him enough to feel the pain he feels for not being what they both wanted him to be. He pleaded that she love him enough to reopen the door to her life and permit him to enter—in spite of his faults and failures. He asked that she remember the good things in their shared past so that together, they could build a future. His words were moving and they touched his daughter, reawakening the love between them.

When people in our lives hurt or disappoint us, it is the love that we remember which removes some of the sting from our wounds. As we recall the time someone sacrificed for us, his or her mistakes and betrayals become less significant. When we remember times of joy and the companionship which blesses our lives, the hurts become less painful and the desire for reconciliation, more powerful.

41

REFRAMING

I recall meeting two men who asked me to officiate at their father's funeral. When we discussed the sentiments and memories to be included in the eulogy, it became obvious that they each remembered their father in different ways. One was angry and bitter and could find nothing good to say about his father. When he envisioned the picture of his family, his father was nowhere in sight. He perceived his father as always working, always disappointing them, and leaving them feeling unimportant and unloved.

His brother's memory was vastly different. Time and time again, he came to his father's defense. The angry son, disturbed with his brother's portrayal of their father, cynically asked, "Did Dad ever take you to a ballgame or was he too busy for that?" His brother responded, "No, Dad never took me to a ballgame, but he often said that he wanted to." Like his brother, he too had been disappointed by their father. But love enabled him to reframe the picture of his father's life, permitting him to see his father from a wholly different perspective. The father he could and reason to love was a man who lived with good intentions. Though he was well aware of his father's failings, he wouldn't permit them to overshadow the goodness he had known.

From my discussions with people who have been able to forgive, it is apparent that one of the important steps on the way to reconciliation is a process therapists call reframing. When there has been enough misery and distress, some people will reconsider the image they have created of the person who wronged them. In his newly framed portrait, the hurts and betrayals no longer overshadow what was good. The art of reframing is knowing what to leave out.

It was historian Arnold Toynbee who observed that a basic rule in writing history is knowing what to omit. According to Rabbi Kassel Abelson, Toynbee learned this lesson from his mother, who was a painter. Watching her paint a watercolor of an old church, he noted that she had not included the weeds which were growing out of the cracks and crevices of the walls. His mother explained that the secret of sketching was in knowing what to leave out. Similarly, one of the secrets of reconciliation lies in knowing what to include and what to exclude as we sketch a portrait of the one with whom we are angry.

Some years ago, Rabbi Pesach Krauss, who served as a Jewish chaplain at Memorial Sloan Kettering Hospital, wrote a book entitled *Why Me? Coping With Grief, Loss and Change*. In it, he describes a technique he uses with cancer patients who are fixated on their pain and personal torment. He shows them a piece of paper with one dot on it and asks them to describe what they see. Many, of course, see the dot, but Rabbi Krauss reminds them that there is far more blank space on the page. He tells them that this space represents all that is precious and good in their life. And he asks that the patients shift their perspective so that the dot is seen for its smallness and insignificance against all of the goodness in life.

Those who forgive still see the dot. The wrongs it represents cannot be erased off the page. But they put the dot in perspective and come to see better than before some of the positive qualities of the other person. The dot may remain and the memory of human imperfections may linger, but the picture has been reframed and what is good now far more prominent.

I heard the story about a man who was told by a friend that his son was too wild. The friend callously remarked, "If he were my son, I would throw him out." Blessed with the ability to see things in their proper perspective, the boy's father replied, "Yes, I would also throw him out if he were your son. But he's my son and not yours. You only see the negative side of him. I also see the positive." It is important to reframe the way we look at others by putting their shortcomings, wrongdoings, and imperfections in the right perspective. It can be the difference between a relationship that is lost forever and one in which forgiveness is found.

Almost everyone we know can be seen in a better light when we develop the art of reframing. In a letter sent by a woman to her former boyfriend, she reveals her ability to search out the good. She wrote, "Dear John, Words cannot express my deep regret at having broken our engagement. Your absence from my side leaves a void which no one can fill. Though you have been overly critical and far too domineering, I forgive you. I'm ready to overlook your cutting remarks and all the other things you do to hurt me. Please let us start over again. I love you. Your adoring Sally . . . P.S.: Congratulations on winning the million dollar lottery!"

JOSEPH AND BENJAMIN

Let's return to the story of Joseph. It reaches its climax when his brothers are forced to respond to a crisis which Joseph precipitates. Emotionally in turmoil, Joseph has to decide whether to forgive or punish his brothers for their treachery. With his identity still hidden, he puts them to a test. He does so by threatening the life of Benjamin, the youngest brother. He hides a priceless silver goblet in Benjamin's belongings. He then turns around, accuses him of stealing it, and threatens to severely punish him.

With Benjamin's fate hanging in the balance, Joseph looks to see how his brothers will react. Would they fail Benjamin as they had Joseph? Or would they care enough to risk themselves for Benjamin? His answer came quickly because, at that moment, the brothers understood that Benjamin's life was in danger and only they could save him.

Alone and away from home, they could have opted to desert Benjamin and simply return to Canaan. Instead, one of the brothers argued passionately and persuasively for Benjamin's freedom. He even willingly offered to suffer punishment in place of young Benjamin.

Suddenly, Joseph saw a side of his brothers he had not known. The ten men who stood before him, united in their concern for Benjamin, had grown and changed over the years. Seeing this transformation, Joseph breaks down and cries. In an emotional catharsis, he reveals himself and forgives his brothers.

Joseph sought to uncover the good in his brothers and he did. From the moment his brothers bravely stepped forward to save Benjamin, Joseph looked beyond the betrayal and hurt he suffered at their hands. From that hard-earned healing perspective, he saw the path to reconciliation and he took it.

SEARCHING FOR A HEALING PERSPECTIVE

In my religious experience, God is portrayed as earnestly desiring to forgive people. For the sake of reconciliation, He does what Joseph had to do to be able to forgive his brothers. Eager to grant forgiveness, God searches for a healing perspective.

In Jewish literature, it is written, "Though 999 angels attest for a person's conviction and only one attests for his defense, God still inclines the scales in his favor." Even after listening to 999 reasons to condemn a person, God seeks the one piece of evidence which will enable Him to see that person in a different light. He searches for the one factor which will overshadow all the negative. Those who desire to be forgiving will never say, "I don't want any part of him any longer." Instead, they will search for that part of a person's character which makes renewing a relationship possible.

In my professional life, I often turn to the collected teachings, *The Ethics of the Fathers*. One sage, Rabbi Joshua, long ago wisely taught that people should "judge every person on the scale of merit." Rabbi Joshua had no doubt noticed a tendency for people to judge others harshly. He observed that people rushed to make a judgment, often overlooking or ignoring insights and information which might enable them to be more sympathetic and understanding.

Rabbi Joshua was urging his students—and all those who would one day read his words—to adopt a different way of judging people. He felt that if we look hard enough, we will find something good and worthy, even in someone who has

wounded or betrayed us. When we look at the whole person and review the totality of the relationship we have shared, surely we can find some reason to seek reconciliation.

Earlier, I wrote of one of God's personal prayers. We're told of another of His prayers in which He prays that He "be inclined to give My children the benefit of the doubt." It is more common to be overly suspicious, condemning, and uncharitable in judging people. But God earnestly looks for some way to judge people favorably. If it can be said that God finds meaning in this simple prayer, then we can as well. We, too, need the willingness to overcome our distrust and cynicism, thereby giving someone the benefit of the doubt.

Some time ago, I came upon the story of a young boy who was flying his kite. The kite went higher and higher until it could no longer be seen. A passerby saw the young boy holding a string and asked him what he was doing. The boy replied, "I'm flying a kite." The man was now perplexed for he saw no kite. And so he asked, "How do you know the kite is up there?" The boy responded by saying, "I can feel it tugging at me."

When we feel a tugging force pulling us toward someone that we have been separated from, it is time to consider reconciliation. The pulling we feel is a force that can take us beyond our anger and enable us to leave the bitterness in our past. Allowing ourselves to give in to this force puts us on the road to restoring a relationship.

Ecclesiastes analyzed life and observed, "There is a time for rending and a time for joining together, a time for silence and a time to speak, a time for hostility and a time for peace." After bonds have been severed by anger, there is a time to reunite those who belong together. After silence has intruded where once there were words, there comes a time to speak.

And after reprisal and retaliation, there comes a time for people to create peace.

RISKING OURSELVES FOR RECONCILIATION

When hurt separates us from someone, it leaves us wondering whether we will ever be able to mend what has been broken. Even though our hearts desire to be reunited, there often is a paralyzing fear of being rejected. There are many people who delay taking the first step, not for want of desiring it, but out of fear of attempting it. Some fear being rebuffed, ignored, or rejected. A crucial step in the path toward forgiveness happens when we convince ourselves that what is important to us is important enough to risk whatever reaction we may face. Far worse than reaching out and being turned away is simply doing nothing and thereby foregoing the possibility of being together again.

One of the most powerful moments in the Book of Genesis comes within the story of Jacob and Esau. The Bible commentaries point out that even prenatally, these two brothers were involved in conflict. In Genesis, we learn of a series of incidents in which Jacob outwits Esau. This creates an impossible atmosphere of antagonism. Their relationship hits rock bottom when Jacob outmaneuvers Esau in order to win the blessing of their father Isaac. Knowing that Esau would seek revenge, Jacob flees. He goes to live with his mother's family in another country. There, Jacob remains for many years, beginning his own family life.

With the passage of time, Jacob begins to feel something tugging at him. The time has come to return home. But Jacob knows that returning home means meeting his brother once again and this is something he dreads. Nevertheless, Jacob makes the long journey back. As he approaches the land of Israel, Jacob learns that Esau is coming out to meet him accompanied by a contingent of 400 men. Jacob fears for his own life, as well as the lives of those in his family and entourage. Quickly, he takes whatever precautions he can to safeguard all of those traveling with him. With preparations made, Jacob spends the night alone—waiting for the next day and his long-postponed encounter with Esau.

One can well imagine how, on that night, Jacob's dread of his powerful brother was mingled with the guilt he had carried for having wronged him years before. Alone in the camp, Jacob is confronted by a stranger. In the most surrealistic encounter in the entire Bible, Jacob wrestles with the stranger all night, stopping only with the approach of dawn.

Many have studied, examined, and reexamined this story. For centuries, people have tried to identify the stranger who wrestled with Jacob. Like others, I have understood this narrative as depicting the struggle going on within Jacob as he prepared to meet his brother. After all the years of separation, the time had come to see Esau once again. And on that night, Jacob wrestled with the guilt he carried and with his own trepidation as to how Esau would receive him.

All night long, Jacob wrestled. Only the first light of dawn signaled to him that darkness had passed. It was time for Jacob to take a step toward reconciliation and possibly, even peace. It was time to walk on, albeit with his fears, his concerns, and his guilt. For years, he had put off this mo-

ment—only to be cut off from his family. Now Jacob understood that only through this encounter could he bring an end to the long night of darkness.

The description of Jacob's meeting with Esau is brief. In chapter 33 of the Book of Genesis, we read of their reunion. There it says, "And Esau ran to meet him and embraced him and kissed him and they wept." Jacob had expected reprisal. The thought of it had frightened him for years. But Esau's first impulse that day was to embrace his brother. For the first time in their lives, there was real affection. At long last, Jacob and Esau were brothers.

The feelings Jacob experienced were all part of the process of reconciliation. Uncertain and nervous about facing the unpredictable, people ask: What if he's still angry with me? How do I let her know how sorry I am? What do I say if he rejects my explanation? What can I do to convince her that I really do forgive her?

I cannot forget one man who was particularly anxious about a long-awaited meeting with his brother. He was well prepared and knew exactly what he was going to say. He had anticipated all the possible responses his brother might have. After they met, he called and said to me, "It's funny, I was so concerned about what I would say. And I was so anxious about what he would say. Until the last minute, I wasn't certain that I could go through with this. And then we saw each other. We both began to cry. We hugged and I knew that everything was going to be fine. Knowing that, above all, we wanted to be together again made it all so much easier."

REACHING OUT

Judith Viorst has collected some wonderful stories of the way in which people ask for forgiveness. One story is of a man named Matthew and his wife, Annie. Matthew had been bedridden with a bad back. Unable to do anything for himself, he is forced to yell for help from Annie. Rather than listening to his yelling, Annie brings him a bell so that he can call to her without shouting. For weeks, Matthew lets Annie know that he needs her by ringing the bell.

When Matthew was healed, their life returned to normal. Within the normalcy of their married life, however, there intruded a terribly nasty fight. It was an argument in which cruel words were exchanged and feelings were hurt. It was one of those fights that are not so easily forgotten. When night came, they went to sleep separately, each of them wondering how they were going to make up. Both Matthew and Annie felt awkward about being the first to speak.

As Annie was tossing and turning in bed, she suddenly heard a sound—that familiar sound of a ringing bell. The bell was the sound of Matthew calling to her, louder and clearer than words could ever tell. "Please come to me. I can't manage without you. I need you." The sound of the bell carried the message that it was time to forgive.

When the time comes to begin mending, we start with a gesture. It can be a word, a symbolic act, a tear, a glance, a note, or anything that says, "Let us be together again." Included within Judith Viorst's collection is a wonderful note written by a young girl who was trying to make up with her mother. Upset that her mother was disappointed with her, the young girl wrote, "Dear Mom, if you stop being mad, I'll start being purfek."

Not surprisingly, the American greeting card industry has entered into the field of reconciliation. Go into any card shop and there are greeting cards which carry the message that it is time for us to be together again. One card reads, "I didn't mean to hurt you—I'm not going to make excuses. I'm just going to ask for your friendship and hope you can forgive me." Another card says, "Let's be friends again—too many foolish mistakes cost us our friendship. Now that time has passed, I know we can put aside our differences." And finally, a more humorous card reads, "I'm not angry—I'm just out of sorts. Please send more sorts."

Not always are these overtures warmly received. There are times when people show no willingness to forgive or be forgiven. For every story of reconciliation, there are many others in which people are never able to create peace. One young man once shared with me how he had tried for years to find just the right way of reaching his father. He never let his father's birthday pass without a card. On holidays, he re-membered him with a gift. And year after year, he received no response. He lived with a broken heart.

One woman whose story I found particularly touching told me of her attempt to reconcile with her son. Years ago, he severed ties with his parents. The woman had explored every possible way of reaching out to him. Painfully, she said, "I've tried to convince myself that our lives would be com-plete with our other children and their children. But I always feel that there is something missing. There's always the empty seat, the birthday that goes uncelebrated, the grandchildren that I'm never going to know."

Fortunately, there are the lucky ones. There are those who reach the point when silence gives way to words as two people seek to bring wholeness back into their lives. Especially in this stage of reconciliation, we can learn something from the story of Joseph and his brothers. When Joseph finally does reveal his identity to them, they are understandably terrified. Joseph, however, no longer has interest in revenge. He wants only to be able to convince them that he is prepared to forgive. And his first words are spoken with tenderness. Joseph says to them so simply, "Please come near to me."

What is important is not only what Joseph said, but how he said it. We are told that he spoke to his brothers softly and gently. This was not the time for open hostility or accusation. Given the opportunity, he approached his brothers in a manner which sought to reassure them that he wanted reconciliation and not retaliation.

THE ART OF LISTENING

There are people who, in Joseph's position, have approached a family member or friend filled with rage. They are determined to use this opportunity to vent their feelings. Seeing this as a time to punish, they unleash a flurry of words and accusations. What could be a time for healing becomes a chance to attack. Words are exchanged, but nothing is heard. There is no new understanding and there is no peace.

Carol Tavris, who has written extensively on anger and its resolution, told of a study conducted by Seymour Feshbach. Feshbach's research studied the interplay between third grade children. He would watch as one child would irritate another.

The children who had been bothered and annoyed were given three ways of handling their anger. The first group was permitted to talk about it with the adults involved in the experiment. Another group was permitted to play with toy guns. And the last group was given a reasonable explanation from the adults for the other child's annoying behavior.

What was it that most effectively reduced the anger of the children who had been bothered and irritated? It was not simply talking about it. Nor was it playing with toy guns. According to Tavris, this study revealed that the most successful way of dispelling the children's anger was for them to come to an understanding of why their classmates had behaved as they did.

This research helps us to comprehend what must be done when two people who have been separated from one another come together for the sake of reconciliation. Their time together is an opportunity to share what caused the anger, the hurt, and the pain. When we communicate in this way, we do so with the hope that the one we are addressing will hear our words and understand what we need from our relationship. When our words are sincere, when they are spoken with consideration for the dignity of the other person, we begin to bring healing and forgiveness into our lives.

Our aim, as Dr. Harold Bloomfield has written in *Making Peace With Your Parents*, is to be able, "without attacking the other person or holding feelings inside, to stand up and say, 'That hurt, here's why and here's what I need so I won't be hurt again.'" Dr. Bloomfield has said that as we approach another person, we do so "from the position of not making them wrong, but rather from, let's try to move through this." Our words and our expressions should, above all, convey that we care and that we want to clear up what has come between us.

Neither pride nor position should be permitted to sabotage the process of reconciliation. This was the concern of the Prophet Malachi who, as pointed out earlier, taught that it is essential that a parent should first seek out a child if necessary. The position and prerogatives of parenthood give way when peace is at stake.

I am indebted to Rabbi David Wolpe who illustrated with insight in his recent book, *The Healer of Shattered Hearts*, what can happen when a parent permits pride and position to intrude in the process of reconciliation. He wrote of the conflict between King David and his son Absalom. Having been estranged from one another, King David sent one of his most trusted advisors to Absalom in order to arrange for a meeting. In the Bible, the description of King David's encounter with Absalom reads this way: "Absalom came to the king and flung himself down on the ground before the king. And the king kissed Absalom."

Rabbi Wolpe pointed out that throughout this encounter, King David is always called the "King." Never is he "Father" to Absalom. According to the biblical record, this was the last time they were to be together and their last chance for reconciliation. At that moment, peace between the two depended upon David turning to Absalom as a loving and concerned father. But David approached Absalom as the king, not as his father. What was needed most was most lacking.

In our attempts to reconcile, we should leave our titles and positions at the door. There they should remain so as not to be permitted to intrude on the process of renewing a relationship.

This is all one young man I knew asked of his father. When he felt that their separation had gone on long enough, he reached out to his father, wanting desperately to begin a dialogue. He was disappointed when he realized that he was dealing with a man who believed that fatherhood entitled him to his son's capitulation. Therefore, the father felt he was absolved from any responsibility to compromise for the sake of reconciliation. When I saw him at his father's funeral, he said sadly to me, "If only he had been willing to meet me halfway."

True reconciliation requires that people be able to listen to one another. Normally, when there is a disagreement, our first impulse is to speak and not to listen. We justify ourselves and close our ears to what is being said to us. When we are more concerned about proving our righteousness than we are about setting right a relationship, the progress toward reconciliation can come to an abrupt stop. As we speak, so must we be able to listen—in order to understand better what has gone wrong and what is necessary to make things right.

One of my colleagues told me of a young man who had called him concerning a problem he was having with his sister. Their parents' estate had been unevenly divided, leaving the young man substantially less than his sister. He had requested that his sister voluntarily equalize their shares of the inheritance. She refused, and justified it by saying that she had been the one to care for her parents and therefore, it was right for her to receive a disproportionately large share of the estate.

Angry both with her and his dead parents, the man vowed he would no longer have any contact with his sister. As time passed, however, he reconsidered and decided that it was more important to have the only person remaining in his family. He invited his sister to meet him for lunch.

After a few moments, their discussion turned to the issue that originally caused their estrangement. Suddenly, both became defensive as they tried to deal with the issue. Once again, she tried to explain why she deserved the money. He, in turn, repeated why he should receive his full portion of the inheritance. Many words were spoken but few were heard. Just when they needed most to listen, they closed their ears. They wouldn't permit themselves to hear the words, pleas, and explanations. And when people refuse to listen to one another, there can be no growth, no change, and ultimately no lasting reconciliation.

While writing this book I saw a revival of Arthur Miller's play, *The Price*. It is the story of two brothers, Victor and Walter Franz, who by chance, meet each other for the first time in years in the apartment of their recently deceased father. The time had come to clear the apartment of the old furnishings. It was also time to clear away the accumulated anger and resentment which had separated them.

Uncomfortable in the presence of his brother, Victor Franz was initially uninterested in talking about the issues that have come between them. Frightened of where the discussion might lead, he was prepared to dismiss it all. Only Walter's persistence led the brothers into a discussion about the wrongs which had been done years ago.

The promise of that moment of candor quickly faded. Each brother was more interested in trading accusations than in genuinely listening to what had turned them away from each other. Both Victor and Walter fought to take the high moral ground. In the end, their meeting had only clarified what it was that separated them. With little willingness to listen and no desire to learn from the past, their encounter only increased the distance which separated them.

Victor's wife Esther looks on in astonishment. She is shocked by what has transpired between the brothers. Towards the end of the play, she reflects, "So many times, I thought the one thing he wanted most was to talk to his brother and that if they could—but he's come and he's gone. It's always seemed to me that one little step more and some crazy kind of forgiveness will come and lift up everyone. When do you stop being so foolish?"

Perhaps Victor and Walter would have been able to take that one little step in their father's apartment if they were willing to work harder at understanding what had made each of them feel so betrayed by the other. Each had preserved his dignity and justified his anger. But sadly, they had also squandered an irretrievable opportunity to reach out, forgive, and reconcile.

A great teacher of ethics once said that if we seek forgiveness from God, we need seeing eyes, hearing ears, and an understanding heart. We need eyes which can clearly see what we have done, ears which can truly hear the words we have spoken, and a heart which can understand the consequences of both our words and our deeds.

The same can be said when we look to bring forgiveness into our lives. We desperately need seeing eyes. We need eyes that will honestly look at ourselves and scrutinize our conduct. We need eyes that are not so blind as to miss what our own role was in shattering a relationship. And we need eyes to look at the other person and remember how much we want him or her to be a part of our lives.

We need ears which will hear what we are saying—and hear also the words spoken to us. And we need ears which will enable us to listen to the despair of those who turn to us seeking forgiveness.

Finally, if there is to be forgiveness, we need as well an understanding heart. We need a heart that can understand the feelings of others. We need a heart that gives us the ability to respond compassionately and wisely to those who turn to us seeking forgiveness.

CHAPTER 5

When There Is No Longer an Endless Series of Tomorrows

"His heart was as great as the world—but there was no room in it to hold the memory of a wrong."

—Emerson

One of the fundamental messages of religion is that life is both precious and limited. It is a psalmist who said, "Teach us to number our days that we may get a heart of wisdom." The wisdom is knowing that life is a finite treasure. Often, however, it is only at a time of serious illness that we come to understand this. It is then, more than at any other time, that people estranged from one another realize the fleeting nature of time—and feel the urgency to seek reconciliation.

Not too long ago, I received an urgent request to visit a patient who was near death. The patient asked that I arrange for his sister to see him before he died. They had argued years ago and then had gone their separate ways. When I phoned the sister, she accepted the invitation and went to his bedside. A few days after her visit, I stopped by to see him. He said, "Thank God I had the time to see my sister. You know, when

I looked at her, I didn't see the same person I had been angry with for so many years. I saw the young girl who had walked with me to school. I saw the young girl who bought me treats whenever she went to the store. I feel better now, but I am left asking myself the same question over and over: 'Why did I wait so long?' ''

This man waited for the same reason most people wait. Never contemplating his own death, he thought that at some time in the future, either he or his sister would make the first move toward forgiveness. But stubbornly, he was unwilling to hasten its arrival.

I have been witness to some remarkable moments of loving reunion. I've been privy to the apologies and embraces which come after years of separation. Few touched me as much as this story of a father and his daughter. Some years ago, I met Bill, who at the time was a patient in the hospital. I had come by to see him several times but he was never in the mood to talk. Bill had recently been told that his condition was terminal. He was despondent and angry. Then one day, he opened up and told me that something was bothering him. Even more than the disease killing him, he was troubled by his relationship with his daughter.

Bill had abandoned his wife and child years earlier. Now he lay dying. He desperately wanted to see his daughter again. But how, after what he had done, could he face her? What would he say? What could he say? Nevertheless, a meeting was arranged with his daughter Linda. She came to visit him in the hospital. As she told me at that time, ''I took one look at my father and so much of my anger began to leave me. I suffered so much because of what he had done. There were times when I hoped that he would suffer for his neglect. But seeing him in the hospital was too much.''

Bill asked his daughter to forgive him. He cried as he spoke of the hurt he had caused her. He looked at Linda and said, "Sometimes we do stupid things in life. I hope you never do something as foolish as I did. All I can do is hope that you believe that there is nothing in my life about which I am sorrier."

Linda could only say, "Dad, I've been angry at you for so long. Do you know what it is like to dream every night that your father would return as mysteriously as he left?" She spent a lot of time with her father in the ensuing weeks. They spoke, held hands, and even smiled.

A few days later, Bill died. When I met with Linda, she told me what had happened during their weeks together. "We told each other, 'I love you.' Do you have any idea what that meant to me? I never thought I'd say those words to my father. And I never imagined that my father would say them to me."

Dying is a lonely process. It becomes lonelier still, when a person faces death feeling the loss of a relationship. For such people and their families, illness is both a tragedy and an opportunity. It is an opportunity to forgive and be forgiven. It is an opportunity to say, "You are not alone." And it is an opportunity to replace loneliness with love.

For several years, I coordinated a telephone outreach service of the New York Board of Rabbis called Project RAV (Rabbinic Answering Voice). People turned to Project RAV looking for advice on personal matters, as well as for information on Jewish law and practice. Many of our callers expressed their heartfelt hope that we might be able to offer suggestions which would help them to restore a broken relationship. They sought practical advice on the steps they could take to bring about reconciliation in their family.

Soon after we began Project RAV, I received a call from

a young man who had AIDS. He was facing death and, at the same time, contending with the conflicts and tensions within his family. Though his brothers and sisters had been wonderful, his father was embarrassed and angry. He could not accept his son's homosexuality. For him, it was an affront to the family honor.

This young man said to me, "My father who always preached to us about family isn't here when I need him. He's ashamed of me and won't see me. I know that I'm going to die. But I don't want it to end like this." He wanted to die with dignity.

The dignity he sought had nothing to do with refusing medical procedures. He was looking for the dignity that comes when a person dies at peace with himself and the people around him. For him, death with dignity was feeling the compassion, kindness, and loving acceptance of his family and friends. Death with dignity was leaving this world knowing that those around him were not standing in judgment of him. What he sought, he did not receive. His father denied him what he needed the most.

As AIDS has become the ruthless killer it is, several monuments have been created to remember its victims. Among them is a colorful patchwork quilt memorializing the thousands of people who have died from AIDS. This quilt has the power to overwhelm those who look at it. Reading the names sewn onto it, you begin to sense the magnitude of this modern plague. One looks at the quilt and wonders many things. How many of these people died feeling that their families considered them an embarrassment? How many died alone and scorned? And how many died sooner than expected because disrupted relationships robbed them of the will to live?

Death with dignity is dying knowing that the gaps in human relationships have been closed and the distances separating people from one another have been narrowed. Dying with dignity is knowing the peace and tranquility that comes when our relationships are in order and in place.

A story is told of still another young man who died of AIDS. The story revolves around the reaction of the young man's father who never accepted or dealt with his son's fatal illness—and certainly never spoke about it. Bob Peterson reacted to his son's AIDS by staying away. He left it up to family members to find excuses for his unwillingness to make a hospital visit.

When his son Brian passed away, Peterson skipped the funeral service and the subsequent memorial rites. Several years later when Peterson died, in clearing out his apartment, his family found cancelled checks made out to institutions involved in AIDS research. Not able to face his dying son, he sought to make amends by contributing to those organizations working on a cure for the disease which had killed him.

Peterson's children found something else. They came upon an emotional letter their father had written. In it, he specified that it was his last request to be buried next to his son. Only in death was he willing to give Brian the closeness that he had denied him in life. For Brian, it was too little and too late. Cancelled checks could not take the place of the love that Brian went without as he faced his death.

Though it is never too late to bring forgiveness to a shattered relationship, it also is never too soon. There is no reason to watch the years pass by before we make a gesture which might bring about reconciliation. Why wait? Why put it off when we know that life is so uncertain and so unpredictable? Now is the time to reach out and recover the people in our lives who have been lost to us. As an anonymous poet once wrote:

> If you're ever going to love me,
> Love me now,
> While I can know,
> The sweet and tender feelings,
> Which from true affection flow.
> Love me now,
> While I am living,
> Do not wait until I'm gone,
> And then have it chiseled in marble,
> Sweet words on ice stone.
> If you ever have tender thoughts of me,
> Please tell me now.
> If you wait until I am sleeping,
> Never to awaken,
> There will be death between us,
> And I won't hear you then.
> So, if you love me,
> Even a little bit,
> Let me know it while I am living,
> So I can treasure it.

CHAPTER 6

Death Is Not the End

"The sweetest revenge is to forgive."

—Isaac Friedman

Death ends a life, but it does not end a relationship. What remains can be either a blessing or a curse. While some are able to look back fondly on the life spent with a loved one, others carry the residue of pain left from years of suffering in a failed relationship. Long after the funeral, they continue to hear the echo of the words which wounded them. A lifetime of feelings linger and refuse to die.

It is during the period of mourning or, more commonly, even much later, that people will tell me of their unresolved feelings and the issues which gave rise to them. Often, they feel that death has left them troubled by the past. The distance which separated them from someone appears magnified and unbridgable in the aftermath of death. Some feel themselves condemned to live forever in the dark shadows cast by a troubled relationship.

Others, however, have refused to be sentenced to a life

in which they know of no peace. Even after death, they seek some kind of reconciliation. For them, it is a welcome last chance to forgive and be forgiven.

Following the death of her father, a woman came to me for counseling. She told a long and sad story of their relationship, recalling countless occasions when she felt ignored and unloved. While growing up, she was envious of the girls whose fathers made time to be with their children. Repeatedly, her father failed to show up at the important occasions in her life. He missed school plays, piano recitals, and graduations. He seemed to have no interest in her or her accomplishments. He made her feel insignificant. And she grew to resent him for it.

Excited to be able to leave her home, this woman went to college filled with optimism. However, during her freshman year, she received a call from her mother informing her that her father had suddenly passed away. She returned for the funeral and remained home with the family for several days. The years which followed his death were filled with painful memories of him. Though he was gone, he was emotionally still very much with her. She often felt lonely and melancholy.

It was during this time that I first met her. She had been visiting with a family affiliated with my congregation. Together, they came to one of the special memorial services we hold four times each year. This service is particularly moving as people gather together to reflect on the memories of loved ones who have passed away.

Something happened to this woman during the service and a short time later, she contacted me and our sessions began. During one of our early sessions, she confided, "I remember the day of my father's funeral. I stood at his casket and cried. I cried because I could only feel bitterness. I cried for the relationship I never had. I cried because I felt anger instead of sorrow. And I cried because I would never be able to have the talk I always wanted to have with my father.''

Having listened to her story, I requested that she return the next week with a photograph of her father. At that session, I took the photograph and placed it on an empty seat in my study. I then asked her to look at it and begin to tell her father those things she wanted to say to him. My suggestion was that she express all the things she wanted to before his death.

Hesitant at first, she began to speak to the photograph as if her father were present. She told him that she had always felt cheated. She said to him, ''All I ever wanted was your love.'' Then, as her emotions overflowed, she walked over to the picture, hugged it, and said, ''This is all I ever wanted. Do you hear me? I wanted to be able to give you a hug.'' She sobbed as she said, ''Daddy, I don't know why you did what you did. I know you didn't do it to hurt me. I just think that you didn't know how to do any better. At least that's what I want to think.''

In preparation for our next session, I asked her to compose a letter from her father. In the letter, I wanted her to have her father explain his actions. She returned with a letter that revealed an important insight into her father's personality. The letter she wrote on his behalf read as follows: ''I wish I knew why I couldn't get close to you. It's not because I didn't love you. There was something within me. I guess I never really felt good about myself. I never felt that I was the kind of father you or your sisters really wanted. I couldn't provide for you what other fathers were giving their daughters. I just never amounted to enough in this world. When I was around you, I felt like a failure. So it was easier, although more painful, to keep my distance. I love you very much and you'll never know how sorry I am.''

She walked over to the picture and said, ''I don't want to hate you anymore. I want to forgive you. So, Daddy, wherever you are—I love you.'' I could see a sense of relief come over her. And I believe she left feeling some inner peace. She had achieved a reconciliation with her past. Though the painful memories remain, they hopefully will never be as painful as they once were.

Another example of reconciliation after death comes from the play *DA*. It is the story of an adult son whose father's passing left unresolved the issues which separated them in life. As the drama begins, the son, Charlie, has returned to Ireland for his father's funeral. With the funeral completed and his obligation fulfilled, Charlie impatiently waits for his flight back to New York. He is anxious to flee his dead father's home as quickly as possible, hopeful that the man he buried would no longer haunt him.

Charlie begins sorting through all the personal effects his father has left behind. And then DA appears. Charlie protests, ''Get out of my head—you're in a box six feet under.'' But as the story of their relationship unfolds, we understand better why Charlie couldn't get DA out of his mind. His memory of DA is wrapped in resentment and bitterness.

As the play draws to its conclusion, it is apparent that their meeting has not been in vain. They talked and listened. Together, they reviewed a lifetime of misunderstanding. Most significantly, for the first time in his life, Charlie was able to develop a fuller understanding of the man he called DA. He realized how much his father's personality had enabled him to become the successful playwright he was. When Charlie returned to New York, DA was still with him. But he was with him as a father, a friend, and a blessing.

Everything we do or leave undone in our lives has its own afterlife. Some of us are left a legacy of love by those who we survive. Others are left to struggle with unpleasant memories and images which will not die a natural death. We are haunted by the scars of deep wounds, feeling pain over and over again as if the wounds were newly inflicted.

In recent years, with increased frequency, we read about people who are so disturbed about where death left a relationship that they are driven to seek reconciliation with those who are no longer alive.

Several years ago, I was told a remarkable story about a father and son who were in the hardware business. For Sam and his son, Kenny, it had been 15 years of hard work. The two had struggled to earn a comfortable living for their families. Sam, who was 62 years old with heart problems, was beginning to think about semi-retirement. Sam's first wife, Marian, died when Kenny was 20. He remarried and his second wife wanted him to take more time off to travel.

Kenny never really liked the hardware business. After a while, he started to think of other work possibilities. At 40 years old, he realized that his life was moving too quickly and unless he made a move, it would soon be too late to pursue a new path.

The father and son got along well together. They laughed a lot and got to know each other beyond the usual father/son relationship. Sure, they had business differences but it never seemed to get in the way of their personal love for each other.

One day, Kenny received a job offer that piqued his interest. He had always hesitated when other opportunities came along. He worried about leaving the security of the family business and the comfortable life he had made for his wife and two young children. Now, he saw this as his last chance to do work that challenged and interested him.

Kenny had to tell his father that he wanted to leave the business and take this new opportunity. Sam was speechless. "How could you leave after all this time together? I always suspected that you weren't really happy in the hardware business, but I thought, through the years, you adjusted to it. Think of your family—you're secure here. You're taking a big risk. What if it doesn't work out? And what about me? You are leaving me at a time that I need you. I need you to run this place. I'm getting older, you know. I need more time off. I need you to stay."

Kenny tried to make his father see his side. He said, "If I don't do this now, it will be too late. I've got one life to live. This is a great opportunity for me. Sure I'm scared and it may not work out, but that's a chance I'll have to take." Kenny saw the sadness in his father's eyes. He loved his father very much so he offered to work part-time nights and weekends to help his father while he took the new job.

The damage had been done though. Sam felt betrayed and rejected Kenny's offer. He told him, "If you are going to leave, go now. The sooner I learn to get along without you, the better."

Kenny tried again to get his father to see his side, but Sam would have none of it. Kenny left feeling hurt, but also feeling guilty. His father had shut him out. He had hoped that his father would have wanted what was best for his son. Instead, his father could only see his own hurt.

Several years passed and Sam and Kenny saw each other only at family gatherings. It was never the same. Sam couldn't get over what he felt was his son's betrayal. Kenny believed he had lost his father's love and began to blame his father for it. Finally, at the age of 68, Sam's heart gave out and he died.

A week after Sam's funeral, on a cold, rainy night, Kenny found himself drawn back to the hardware store where he toiled for years with his father. The old place had not changed much. He walked into a room that he and his father shared as an office. The familiar odor of Sam's cigar still lingered in the air. Kenny went to his old desk and—to his surprise— found almost everything still in its place.

Out of the corner of his eye, Kenny spotted several pic- tures on the wall. He slowly walked over to them. One was a photo of himself and his father in the store by the cash register. He had his arm around his Dad's shoulders and they were both smiling. Kenny then smiled sadly to himself. He looked at another photo of himself with his father and his daughter, Diane. The three of them were playing ball at Sam's house in the yard. Kenny turned to sit down and found himself at Sam's desk. A flood of memories and emotions came back to him.

He remembered the day he told his father he was leaving. He could still hear himself explaining why he had to leave. He felt that he could be a devoted son and still go his own way. He also remembered the painful words of rejection his father spoke that day.

Kenny thought, "Dad, I'm sitting at your desk feeling hurt and feeling guilty." He pounded on the desk. No longer able to contain himself, he cried out, "If only you had given me a chance, we could have worked it all out."

Kenny's anger subsided. He began to cry. Through his tears, he said aloud, "Dad, I want you to know that whatever I did, I never meant to hurt you. I'll never stop missing you. Please forgive me if I failed you in any way." Having said these words, Kenny felt transformed. For a moment, he felt as if he were in his father's presence. In the power of that moment, it seemed as though his father said to him, "Son, I forgive you. I love you. Please forgive me."

Kenny remained in the office for a few moments longer. As he was leaving, he turned to close the door behind him. He took one more look and said, "Goodbye Dad. I love you. I forgive you."

For a long time, Kenny wondered whether he would ever be able to forgive his father. When he returned to their office, something within him understood that by forgiving, he was leaving behind hurtful memories.

This is a story that tells us how love can create a bridge that scales the boundaries of death. In so doing, it offers us the possibility of a transcendent moment of reconciliation.

Within my own tradition, there are many rituals which guide the mourner through a time of loss and bereavement. In an act of remembrance and faith, the mourner says a prayer called the Kaddish each day. At every prayer service, the mourner stands in the presence of the congregation and utters the timeless words of this humbling prayer. These words have been spoken by Jewish mourners throughout the ages. With each word, the mourner is drawn to thoughts of shared moments with the deceased.

I've been told that the recitation of the Kaddish becomes a vehicle for reconciliation with a deceased relative. A member of my congregation, in sharing his experience, related this story: "So much distance separated my brother and I when he died. We were not at all alike. He was only concerned with what he could take from my parents. He had time for nobody unless you could do something for him. I can't tell you how much it bothered me. I wanted a brother and my parents wanted a son.

harles Klein

"When he was killed, I was confused. More than mourning his death, I mourned the relationship we had lost. And then my father asked me to say the Kaddish for my brother. It was the last thing I wanted to do. But I knew I could not disappoint my father who was too ill to do it himself.

"I was angry when I began coming to services to say the Kaddish. I didn't want to do this for my brother who had so little time for me. But then, after a few weeks, I stood up and said to my brother, 'Steve, I'm making time for you. Now you make time for me.' I told him how hurt I had been over the years.

"From that time on, I would use the special moments in prayer as an opportunity to review our relationship. On the last day of saying Kaddish, I stood up and I said to him, 'Steve, we've talked more during these few weeks than in the last 15 years. Along with all the disappointments, I've been able to remember some of the wonderful times we spent together. Today I think of you and remember the brother who grew up with me. I'm sorry for what we missed. But I think I have achieved a better understanding of what you were looking for in life and why.' "

This member of my congregation went on to say to me, "I read that by saying Kaddish, the mourner helps his deceased loved one to enter into heaven. Rabbi, I don't know if that's true. But I can tell you that I felt a little bit of heaven the day I walked out of that chapel knowing that, at long last, I had found some peace with my brother."

We all know people who remain stuck in the valley of the shadow of death. There they dwell—angry, bitter, and resentful of what was done to them and what was not done for them. The stories I've heard and the people with whom I've worked have helped me to understand that when we try to forgive those who are gone from our lives, we begin to take our first steps out of that dark valley. And we emerge from that valley when we can say, as Kenny said to his father, Sam, "I forgive you. I understand."

COPING WITH SUICIDE

There is a special intensity to the anger felt when the one who is gone forever has committed suicide. The grief that is experienced by the survivors is sometimes intermingled, and even overshadowed, by their rage. The person who has committed suicide has taken one life, but destroyed many others. Suicide dramatically transforms the lives of those who survive, leaving them lonely and filled with doubt and shame.

The depth of anguish and anger is reflected in the following story. It is about a woman named Barbara and her son Howard, who committed suicide. Several weeks after the incident, Barbara came to see me. She began our session by saying, "I've been waiting to speak with someone. I feel like I'm going to burst. For the past few weeks, I've listened to everybody tell me how terrible it is that my son is gone. And all the time, I've wanted to scream. How could Howard do this to me? They don't understand what it's like to be the mother of a son who committed suicide. He's not just gone— he killed himself.

"When people look at me, I wonder if they're saying, 'How could you not have known something was so wrong with your son?' I'm angry at him for copping out. I'm angry at him for making me feel like a failure—for making me feel like I failed as a parent. He's dead now, but for the rest of my life, I'll question how it was that I didn't see what was happening.

"No one knows what it feels like to think yourself responsible for something like this. Since he was found dead, I've carried this weight around, wondering if there was something I did that made Howard do this.

"Why couldn't he come to me? I would have done anything to get him help. And I'm angry because I had a life and he took that from me. How am I ever going to live again? How am I ever going to laugh again? How could he do this? Inside me, I feel like a volcano ready to blow. There is so much anger and hostility and rage. I just have to let it out."

Over the sessions that followed, Barbara did let out her anger and rage. Listening to her and others who have survived the suicide of a loved one can be a painful experience. How heavy is the burden they carry. How difficult it is to go on in life when the death of someone else has raised the possibility that we failed to do what might have been done to prevent a tragedy. There is tremendous anger that the fabric of life has been torn and it will never be whole again.

Ultimately, survivors of suicide need to find a way to forgive those who have committed suicide. Until they can forgive, they won't be able to fully mourn. So long as they carry the feelings of anger and the sense of having been betrayed, they cannot begin the process of grieving the actual death. Forgiveness is the key to moving on. But how—how does someone forgive and go forward in the aftermath of such tragedy?

Often, those who survive a suicide find it beneficial to turn to a grief counselor. One of the most significant and necessary aspects of grief counseling is enabling the survivor to understand more fully the anguish and torment of the loved one who ended his or her life. The grief counselor will attempt to guide the person to the realization that the suicide was not intended to wound those who survive. Rather, as incomprehensible as it might be, it was the only path which seemed to promise relief from the misery and pain of living. Only by understanding the enormous anguish of the one who ended life can those who survive realize that, for some people in the depths of misery, the single concern is finding a way out. And with this awareness comes the possibility to forgive.

Some can find forgiveness of a loved one's suicide without the benefit of counseling. One survivor said to me, about a year and a half after the suicide of her husband, "For months, I mourned for me. I mourned all that I had lost. I mourned the fact that I was evidently not the wife I should have been. And I was angry at my husband for taking everything away that was important to me. I once went to his grave and screamed at him for doing this to us.

"And then I listened. I listened for a voice that would explain why it had to be this way. For those few moments, I listened better than I had ever done before. As I stopped thinking of myself, I could hear my husband pleading with me to understand the problems he found so unsolvable and the pain he felt so intolerable. As I thought of his torment, my own became less important. And as sad, as terribly sad as I am, I can no longer be angry with him. I can only love the man I loved so much and forgive him for what he did. Now I'm no longer mourning for me—I'm mourning for him."

Those who have carried bitter memories know how difficult it is to live while still weighed down by the pains of the past. Only when they have found a way to forgive can they appreciate the truth found in the words of the poet Percy Shelley. He wrote in his poem, *Prometheus Unbound*, "Among which the things which make us good, great, joyous, beautiful and free, is to forgive wrongs darker than death or night."

CHAPTER 7

Why Did I Wait So Long?

"Wisdom oftimes consists of knowing what to do next."
—Herbert Hoover

Many of us live our lives believing that there are an endless number of tomorrows which will make it possible to do in the future what ought to be done today. Some wait for the time to be ripe, only to find out that time can become overripe. Often, we wait too long to speak to those we have hurt or offended. Though our words have been formulated for years, we hesitate to say what we know we must. We wait for tomorrow, never expecting that death might rob us of the opportunity to enjoy a reconciled relationship.

The phone call which tells of the death of a relative or friend is, for some, a notice that they have run out of tomorrows. Mourning a death becomes compounded by the difficult questions which do not die. They are the questions I hear so frequently. People wonder, "Why did I wait so long? Why didn't I clear up what had come between us years ago? Why couldn't I say I was sorry? Why did I have to keep putting things off?''

Death takes a life from us and for some, it leaves unresolved feelings of guilt and shame. There is guilt over something which was done or left undone, or something said or left unsaid. And there is shame, because an effort to heal a relationship was never made.

Those who wait too long often feel a need to find a way back to the one who is gone forever. All they want is a moment—one brief moment—to speak the words which would explain why they acted as they did. They yearn for one moment to apologize for what was done to diminish a special relationship. They want one last opportunity to express regret for having been less than what was expected of them. Too often, I have looked into someone's eyes only to see suffering. I've watched as people have stood beside a casket and I felt the ache of those who waited for a tomorrow which never came.

Their thoughts were expressed by a woman who sobbed uncontrollably at her father's casket as she said to me, ''I thought the time would come—I wanted so much for us to be together. Now, here I am crying at his funeral. Crying not only because he is gone—but because I waited and I lost my chance. My father was so young at heart. I thought he would live for years and that we would one day talk. How can I live with myself now? The pain is unbearable. Why did I wait?''

The pain of lost opportunity is again expressed in the story of three adult children who spoke with me prior to their father's funeral. Their father had abandoned them long ago. One day, he tried to reconcile with them. Resentful, they refused all contact with him. As the years went by, he often tried to reach out, but their resistance did not soften. Now, they realized that even though he had let them down, they would have to live with the burden of knowing that they had denied him the chance to make amends. They held each other and cried, having come to understand that they waited too long. When they were younger, they could speak of how their father had failed them. But now, they knew that they had to accept their responsibility for a failed relationship.

Though someone is gone from your life forever, what lingers on is the need to be released from the torment which comes from knowing you have failed that person. Those who recall the narrative in the Book of First Samuel, which describes the relationship of King Saul and the Prophet Samuel, remember that a very crucial period in the history of Israel, the newly appointed king disappointed and disobeyed the Prophet. He had failed to measure up to the responsibilities entrusted to him. King Saul had let the Prophet Samuel down and the Prophet offered no way of setting things right. A man marked for greatness, King Saul lived his life tortured and distressed because he had not lived himself worthy in the eyes of Samuel.

Samuel's death did not bring an end to King Saul's guilt. In a time of national emergency, Saul went to consult with the spirit of Samuel. King Saul wanted most of all to be told by Samuel that all had been forgiven. He wanted to hear the words which would tell him that Samuel had approved of the changes which would tell him that Samuel had approved of the changes which had taken place in his character. All of us know people who empathize with what King Saul was feeling. For them, the death of the person they wronged seems to foreclose on any possibility of finding forgiveness.

Several years ago, I began counseling a woman named Susan. Though she loved her mother, she had permitted their relationship to deteriorate over the years. She told me, "I did something terrible. When my mother remarried, she became extremely close with her husband's daughters. Over the years, I became jealous. It seemed to me that she had come to consider them as her own daughters.

"I was hurt and I decided that I would let her know what it feels like when someone you love makes it seem that you have been replaced. I became very close with one of my aunts, treating her more like a mother than an aunt. I went to her with my problems. I made certain that my mother would know that my aunt was the one in whom I confided. Over the years, I would look at my mother and know that she was hurt by what I was doing. It seemed that my plan was paying off. She was finding out how I felt.

"As the years went on, I wanted to stop all of this. Yet I didn't know how to go to her and ask her forgiveness. And then one day, my stepfather called and told me that my mother had died. My first thought was that now it is too late. She's gone and I can't bear the fact that I never said I'm sorry to her. I know that what I did came in retaliation and now it seems so very senseless. I did wrong and I feel so guilty. But what's worse is that I can't believe it's too late. I don't want to have to carry this my whole life."

Although it was too late for Susan to renew a relationship, it was not too late to find forgiveness. I suggested that she write a letter to her mother in which she assumed responsibility for her actions. If Susan was to find forgiveness, it would come by honestly looking at herself and what she did wrong. I then advised her to take that letter to her mother's funeral. I asked that she find some time to be alone with her mother before the memorial service. She was to read the letter and place it in the basket.

When I saw Susan during the period of mourning, she said to me, "As I read that letter and asked for my mother's forgiveness, I realized something very important. Knowing my mother and the kind of person she was, I felt that somewhere she was looking at me and saying, 'You're forgiven.' I felt her love and pray she felt my love for her."

It is common for members of the clergy to counsel people who are still troubled by a feeling of unresolved guilt months or even years after the death of a relative. At times, it seems that acts of commission or omission loom larger as the days pass by. Although living in the present, they are still reliving a past in which they violated a relationship. Often, they come with a compelling need to speak about the wrong they did. Something inside cries out for expression and closure.

This sentiment was experienced by a psalmist in the Bible. His gnawing need to unburden himself led to these words:

> When I kept silence, my bones wore away
> Through my groaning all the day long.
> I acknowledge my sin unto you
> And my iniquity I have not hid.
> I said: "I will make confession concerning my
>   transgressions unto the Lord."
> And You forgave the iniquity of my sin.

Some say that silence is golden. Yet gold can turn to dust when we avoid saying the words which we know must be spoken. Weary of the silence, people will turn to someone months and even years later to tell of the hurt they caused.

When Joe came to see me, two years had already passed since his wife's death. During the years of their marriage, Joe's wife had complained bitterly that he was inattentive to her and the family. He was a workaholic. Rarely did he have time for her or their children. He would become angry when she asked that he set aside more time for the family. When she passed away, Joe was left feeling that he had cheated her. He realized that he had not been present for his wife who had loved him. Everywhere he saw a couple together, he became miserable as he thought of the ways in which he had neglected and hurt his wife.

On the day that I met Joe, he said to me, "I feel lousy. It's bad enough I ruined my life. But I also ruined Karen's. I didn't give her the companionship she wanted. I should have wanted the same things from our marriage. When she begged me for some attention, I would become angry. Can you imagine I became angry because she wanted my love? It's hard to live with myself. She's gone two years and I still can't stand myself for disappointing her. If only I would have listened to her."

We continued to speak of all the things that Joe regretted. He went on, recalling so many times that he looked at his wife's disappointed face. Her death only accentuated the guilt he felt for creating the distance which separated them. Often, he wondered aloud why he had been unwilling to become the kind of husband his wife deserved. All he wanted was "one more chance to make things right."

Joe couldn't erase the record of the life that he shared with Karen. But there was still an opportunity to repair his relationship with his children. I asked him to arrange a joint session with them. At that meeting, he was to tell them all the things he regretted about his relationship with Karen and with them. I wanted him to help his children understand how disappointed he was in himself as a husband and a father. And

84

most significantly, I hoped that Joe might express his desire to become the kind of father Karen wanted him to be.

Joe's conversation with his children was a powerful experience. As he spoke, he purged himself of some of his pain. He shared with me that, as he was speaking with his children, he imagined that his wife was with them. Joe was taking some very important steps and he felt strengthened as he spoke— believing that his wife was looking on approvingly.

Some months later, Joe called me. He told me of the times that he had been spending together with his children and their families. He was obviously filled with joy knowing that he was doing something that Karen always wanted. Joe said, "Being able to do things with my children has made a difference in my life. I can't make up for all the opportunities I missed with Karen, and I know that I missed out on a lot. But when I'm with my children, I feel that Karen knows that I'm trying to be the kind of person she always wanted me to be."

There is no doubt in my mind that people can benefit by writing the letters and speaking the words which tell of their sorrow and regret. The act of expressing regret and remorse is absolutely fundamental for those who look for forgiveness. And yet I suspect there is a need to do more. To forgive oneself, one must go beyond words. There must be action, deeds, and new commitments which show that remorse has led to growth and change. When, like Joe, we take the steps to become the kind of person our loved one had hoped we would become, we begin to feel forgiven. As we strive to be more than we are, we can be more forgiving of the person we once were.

Sometimes, the death of a loved one leaves us tormented. We lament the times we were neglectful, and are dispirited remembering the occasions when we were less than what was expected of us. At these times, some hear a voice from within. It points them toward the path of reconciliation.

This was the voice I thought Ray Kinsella was hearing as I sat and watched the movie *Field of Dreams*. Those who recall the movie will remember that Ray began to hear a voice telling him, "If you build it—he will come." What he was hearing, I believe, was something inside calling him to make peace with his father who had died years before. Some time had passed since his father's death and Ray was still troubled by the way he had treated his father in their last years together.

Long ago, Ray had left both his home and his father. Apparently, he was disappointed that his father had permitted age to rob him of his dreams. When Ray turned 36, he began to sense that he had been too judgmental of his father. I think Ray began to look at his own life and he realized how easy it was to lose one's dreams. This made him feel strangely unsettled. He regretted the lost opportunities. Most significantly, I believe he regretted that he made himself a stranger to the father who loved him.

The mysterious voice which called to Ray was telling him that what he wanted most was a reunion with his father. I feel it was that voice that ultimately guided him back to his father. For a few magical moments, Ray and his father were reunited. They tossed a ball back and forth just as they had done years ago. In that simple game of catch played by countless fathers and sons, there was reconciliation.

How Ray wanted that moment to linger! He had found the man who was his father, and he had the opportunity to make things right with him. Ray treasured those precious moments. Together, they were writing a new end to their story.

As they tossed the ball back and forth, the smiles on their faces said to me that a father had forgiven the son and the son had forgiven himself. They had found each other in reconciliation.

That one scene in the movie touched me as it did millions of people. When the movie was first released, it was not uncommon for men and women to remain in their seats crying long after the film had ended. Was it because the movie reminded them of the distances they had permitted to develop with people they loved? I think so. I think they cried with sorrow. They cried for themselves and a few cried with hope that perhaps one day, they, too, would be forgiven.

In the most famous of all the psalms, there is a verse which has comforted generations of mourners. The psalmist said, "Yea, though I walk through the valley of the shadow of death, I feel no harm, for You are with me." These incomparable words bring a message of hope to those who have lost a loved one. Knowing the anguish of the mourner, the psalmist spoke of hope and faith. For it is a lonely walk through the valley. And the walk is made longer and lonelier when regret and remorse fill the heart of the mourner.

For those who are troubled by mistakes they may have made, the valley can seem as if it is without an end. Expressing regret and remorse, seeking forgiveness, and settling the accounts left unsettled at the time of death hold out the promise of reconciliation which leads us through the valley and back into life.

CHAPTER 8

To Care Enough to Bring Peace

"No matter what accomplishments you achieve, somebody helps you."

—Althea Gibson

Included in the Jewish morning prayer service are several selections from one of the codes of Jewish law. My favorite is a teaching which offers guidance to those who want to live a life of lasting significance. Along with a strong cup of coffee, these words of instruction wake us up to life each day: "These are the things which bring fulfillment to a person in this world and promise eternal reward. They are: giving honor to father and mother, acts of kindness to people in need, attendance at the house of study, hospitality to the wayfarer, visiting the sick, providing for the orphan bride, showing respect to the dead, absorption in prayer, bringing peace between people, and the study of the law is equivalent to them all."

Each morning, the words of this teaching are a reminder that life is both measured and made meaningful by acts of kindness, loyalty, and devotion which take us beyond empathy and lead us into the lives of others. It suggests that those who wish to leave their mark on the world must begin with the small corner they inhabit. This teaching cuts a pathway through life for all those in search of direction and purposeful living. It asks that people make time for honoring parents, visiting the sick, caring for the homeless, and dealing charitably with those for whom life has been a struggle for basic existence.

The anonymous sage, whose wisdom this teaching reflects, has included within this list something which may surprise many of us. Accustomed as we have become to the modern day admonition that we "mind our own business," few would consider it a personal responsibility to work at bringing peace between people.

Our culture has successfully persuaded us to believe that the quarrels of others are not our concern. From the movies we see, the television shows we watch, the books we read, and the lives of people we observe, we have come to accept that shattered relationships are the price we pay for living in a difficult and demanding world. People appear more willing than ever before to move on in life while leaving behind broken relationships. Few of us feel the urgency to include within our agenda the task of bringing peace between people.

The sage's choice of commandments was quite deliberate. He included the obligation of working to bring peace between people because he believed that intervention into personal problems is not the intrusion people perceive it to be. For him, it is an act of loving kindness. It is the response of a family member or friend who is unwilling to accept broken relationships.

And yet, it is even more than this. The peacemaking efforts we perform in our homes, our families, and our communities are part of the responsibility God has given us in the ongoing work to perfect the world. When we work to create harmony where there is discord, we in effect become God's emissaries, bringing His light where we know it is sorely needed. Though we pray to God for peace, my tradition asks that people understand that it is up to each one of us to work in partnership with Him so that peace may be brought into everyone's lives.

A colleague of mine spoke of the gratification he felt in fulfilling this commandment. Shortly before the High Holy Days, he received a call from a congregant distressed over the feuding which was tearing his family apart. My colleague, who over the years had come to know this entire family arranged for a meeting in his office. As the session got under way, one of the invited participants commented, "Rabbi, surely you have more important things to do before the High Holy Days!" The rabbi responded by saying, "In fact, I have many important things to do, but nothing is more important to me than restoring peace to this family. If I can bring you back together, then I have accomplished something of lasting significance."

Our sage was not a lone voice urging people to actively work at bringing peace. Many stories of my tradition emphasize the importance of this caring act. One of these stories tells of a rabbi who met the Prophet Elijah in a crowded marketplace. Feeling certain that in the market there would be good people who had lived righteously, he asked Elijah, "Who here in this marketplace has lived a life which qualifies them for Godly rewards?"

Elijah pointed to two men walking in the crowd of people. Eager to find out what distinguished these men, the rabbi ran over and asked, "What are your special merits in life?"

The men looked at each other and answered, "We have no special merit unless it be that when people are in trouble, we comfort them and when they quarrel, we make them friends again."

That it was Elijah who found special merit in this aspect of their life's work should not surprise us. According to the Prophet Malachi, the coming of the Messiah awaits a world which will be made ready by Elijah. It is Elijah's responsibility to create the conditions which will prepare the world and its people for the Messianic Day. Elijah would first "turn the hearts of the fathers to the children and the hearts of the children to the fathers." Though he was given a host of tasks to accomplish, this was certainly the most challenging.

Unstated, but embedded within the legend of Elijah, is a realization that before there can be universal peace founded upon respect and appreciation of different ways, Elijah will first have to inspire people to seek reunion with family members and friends. For as long as people willingly accept the brokenness of precious relationships, there can be no hope for a worldwide day of healing and peace. Elijah's task was to bring peace between people, hopeful that the hearts he would turn toward loved ones would then turn toward others in the world.

All around us is evidence of shattered relationships. Who doesn't know family or friends who have been touched by this pain? Their distress calls out for more than a shrug of our shoulders. Someone near to us is hoping that we will not calmly accept their torment. They look for a friend who will enter their lives and strive to bring peace.

Historian Thomas Fleming tells us how friends intervened on behalf of Thomas Jefferson and John Adams in an effort to restore their friendship. The two had been close friends until Jefferson defeated Adams, thereby denying him a second term as president in the year 1800. When Jefferson went to pay a visit to Adams in the White House, he was greeted with raging anger. Adams began screaming, "You turned me out, you turned me out."

For eleven years, they did not speak. And then, after the anger had subsided somewhat, the work of reconciliation began. Friends of the two men noticed a change in both Jefferson and Adams. When one man visited with Adams, the former president said, "I loved Jefferson and I still do." Those words were brought back to Jefferson, who in turn asked that Adams know how much their friendship meant to him. Soon, the two men were corresponding on a wide range of topics. They forgave each other and renewed their friendship. The time had come for peace. Friendship was restored because people cared enough to intervene.

Most of us do not have to look far to find a relationship in need of healing. Someone we know awaits the caring response of a peacemaker. When such intervention occurs, it holds out the promise of reconciliation and lasting reward for the one who brought it about.

CHAPTER 9

A Second Chance

"All growth is the result of risk taking."

—Jude Wanniski

O n the road to reconciliation, there are always doubts and reservations. Many people have shared with me their disbelief in the possibility of real change occurring within the person who hurt them. Influenced by our culture, which has made many of us skeptical about people's capacity to change, they protest in familiar terminology that "You can't teach an old dog new tricks" or "A leopard doesn't change its spots."

Change, however, does happen. People are able to take control over their lives, confront their mistakes, and renew themselves. In response to people's cynicism, I often share the parable frequently told by clergymen about a king who had a precious stone widely renowned for its beauty. One day, he accidently dropped the stone. When he picked it up, he discovered that there was a hairline crack on its surface.

There was no hope of repairing it until one jeweler volunteered to attempt this difficult task. The jeweler worked feverishly for one month. When he finished his work, he announced that the stone had been repaired. The king looked closely at the stone and began to marvel at the jeweler's handiwork. The hairline crack on its surface had been transformed into a long and delicate stem at the top of which was a rose carved out by the jeweler.

The moral of this parable? Isn't it telling us not to give up on somebody because of an imperfection, a transgression, or a failing? People can leave behind a past which is both escapable and nonbinding. As a crack in a stone can become a flower, so, too, can an imperfection in a person give way to virtue.

One of the most moving stories of the Bible is found within the very short book of the Prophet Hoshea. We learn that Hoshea married a woman named Gomer who later deserted him for another man after giving birth to Hoshea's three children. Though he was deeply hurt by his wife's unfaithfulness, Hoshea did not become embittered. And when instructed by God to take Gomer back into his life, Hoshea complied. Hoshea's demands upon Gomer were few. As he restored her to his home, he requested only that "You must dwell as mine for many days—you shall not play the harlot, or belong to another man, so will I also be to you."

Hoshea was not asked to forget the hurt Gomer had done to him. He was asked only to suspend his disbelief and to put aside whatever doubts he had that Gomer could become better. Hoshea was asked to believe that Gomer could and would one day emerge as a new person, her life refashioned and recreated.

The story of Hoshea transforms the act of giving a person a second chance into a divine imperative. For the sake of family, for the sake of all that mattered, Hoshea was commanded to give Gomer a second chance. Following the biblical narrative in its entirety, you would see that built into its view of human relations is the realization that relationships of family and friendship cannot survive unless someone is prepared to grant another person a second chance. The command first heard by Hoshea has echoed down through the ages. It speaks to us today, reminding us that when all is said and done, we give someone a second chance because it is simply the right thing to do.

The challenge Gomer confronted cannot be overstated. The task of changing and bettering ourselves is a test of our resolve. Some stumble and some fail as they work at renewing themselves. But for others, there is growth, movement, and real change. In my work, I have been able to observe that more often than not, those who change are able to do so because they feel the love and support of family and friends.

There is a vast difference in motivation between those who are threatened with the words, "change, or else," and those who are lovingly informed, that "though you hurt me—I still believe in you and I know you can become better." With the first words, one feels fear and intimidation; with the other words, warmth, encouragement, and support. Intimidation only creates anxiety, uncertainty, and a sense of inadequacy.

When we give someone we care about an opportunity to change, it should be given as suggested by the philosopher Martin Buber—in the spirit of "confirming the other." As we turn to someone who has disappointed us and say, "I believe in you and I recognize in you the person you have been created to become," we are doing more than simply offering the person another chance. We are giving someone a reason to believe in his or her capacity for growth.

On more occasions than I wish to recall, I have sat with

families and listened as someone demanded that there be "change, or else." How often I have heard the ultimatum, "If he doesn't change, we're finished," or "If she doesn't begin to understand my needs better, I'm leaving." "Change, or else" is not a second chance. It is a threat spoken with the voice of power and not love. If change is never easy, an ultimatum only serves to make it more difficult.

People respond more positively to love than to intimidation. They don't readily change, but those who do, often do because they know there is someone hoping for them, standing with them, believing in them, and even praying for them.

How powerfully this was portrayed in the novel *Les Miserables* by Victor Hugo. As the story begins, we meet Jean Valjean, who has been sent to a prison labor camp. Having served his time, Valjean was paroled from prison. He desires only the opportunity to start life anew. However, the people he meets refuse to give him the chance he needs to begin over again.

Only the compassion and concern of a Catholic bishop rescues Valjean from a life of misery. Feeling the bishop's support and sensing the bishop's faith in him, he commits himself to becoming better. The bishop did for Valjean what nobody else would. He made Valjean aware that he believed in his potential to be more than he had been. It is such faith and belief that can be the difference between a life which is spent rehearsing the mistakes of the past and a life dedicated to reversing them.

There is a teaching in the Ethics of the Fathers which urges that we, like the Catholic bishop in Victor Hugo's novel, "not give up on anyone—for every person has his hour." The most precious gift we offer people who have disappointed us and perhaps themselves as well, is our confidence that their hour will yet come. Knowing that there is a person willing to stand by even as others turn away is all that some people need in order to change.

Those who have received such a gift do not quickly forget the supporting role played by others who willingly and compassionately gave them an opportunity to grow. At the time of his mother's funeral, one man told me of the enormous impact his mother had on his life. During his college days, he went from school to school. He was failing everywhere he went. As he said, "I wasn't feeling very good about myself then. I disappointed my parents and didn't show them the kind of respect they deserved. People were giving up on me. My father, my teachers, and even my friends began to see me as a loser.

"One person stood by me. I recall one day when I was particularly abusive to my mother. She said to me, 'I don't care what you say to me or how you treat me. All I want is for you to hear what I'm going to say to you now. You're more than you think you are and more than others think you are. I know better than anyone what you're made of—and you're good stuff.' "

The man continued, "I pretended as though I didn't hear her. After all I had done to her, I didn't deserve what she was giving me. My mother gave me a lot of things in life—but the best thing she ever gave me was that feeling I had that day. Knowing what she felt and how she thought, I began to think that I could do things differently. Everything I've become in life is a result of that woman who gave me a second, third, fourth, and fifth chance when others gave up on me."

I once heard a story of a wife who had gone to see her rabbi to discuss a persistent failing of her husband. The rabbi took the woman to a window where they watched as a small child was learning to walk. The child took a step and fell down. Time after time, the child's mother helped him to get up—only to watch him fall again.

The rabbi said to the woman, "Eventually the child will walk. One day, the child will not fall and his poor mother won't have to pick him up any longer. The same is true for your husband. One day, he will become the husband you want—one day, he'll stand on his own two feet. Until then, he needs your faith and encouragement."

Few people I've met really want to persist in a life of falling down and failing those they care about. Most people have a desire to grow beyond the mistakes of the past. Growth, transformation, deeper relationships, and the desire to live a better life are what many people think and even dream about. But as we may know from personal experience, it is much easier to renew a license or an insurance policy than it is to renew ourselves. Changing ourselves requires inner strength, discipline, and commitment. It also requires the presence of someone who shares a vision of what we can become and who is prepared to support us, encourage us, and pick us up along the way.

Surrounding the city of Jerusalem is a wall with eight gates. Each gate has a name and a history. The one most recently added has appropriately been called The New Gate. In life as well, there are many gates. Throughout our days, gates are opening and closing.

Is there someone you care about whose life is in need of renewal? Then let that person know that in everyone's life, there is a new gate. Convince him or her by your trust and confidence that this gate is accessible. And then stand by as the person walks through the gate into what will hopefully be a new life for both of you.

CHAPTER 10

Reconciliation Day

> "May He who has brought peace to the heavens above bring peace to us."
>
> —The Prayerbook

American culture has created a special day for giving thanks, as well as days dedicated to mothers, fathers, grandparents, teachers, and secretaries. There is a day for remembering those who died in war and a day for recalling the founding of this nation. There is a day for presidents and a day for labor.

Knowing that there was a need for at least one more special day, Ann Landers used her nationally syndicated column to promote the idea of a reconciliation day. Having spent much of her time advising people how to heal the brokenness in their lives, she asked that they set aside a reconciliation day for forgiveness and reunion. For those readers of her column who responded to her call, reconciliation will long be remembered as a day of renewal and joy.

Some of Ann Landers' readers shared their reconciliation day experiences. One thankful young man wrote, "My brother and I were born 20 months apart. Mom dressed us alike and many thought we were twins.

"Tommy was better at basketball, but I was better at soccer. He played a great trombone and I was pretty good on the drums. I was lousy in English and he did my homework. He wasn't so hot in math so I helped him out. We were competitive like most brothers, but there were never any serious fights or arguments. The only big falling out was over a girl. Tommy was nutty about her but she liked me better.

"It was understood my brother and I would go into the family business started by our grandfather. We knew something about it, having worked there most summers since we were teenagers. Tommy (being older) went in first. I decided to take a year off after college and travel. While I was in South America, Dad died suddenly of a heart attack. When I came home for the funeral, I got the shock of my life. He did not have a will. Mom inherited everything. She was very fond of Tom's wife and didn't care much for mine. So the long and short of it was that I was out of luck.

"My wife and I decided to move out of town, borrow some money from her father, and start our own business. We cut all family ties. Ten years passed. Mom died. We didn't go to her funeral. I was angry and bitter, feeling I'd been cheated. Two weeks ago, I received a copy of your column on reconciliation from Tommy. Across the top, he had written, 'I miss you, please call me.' That very evening, I called and we both cried. The following weekend, he and his wife and their two kids came to see us. It was my birthday. That was the greatest gift I have ever received in life."

When we hear stories such as this one, we realize how terribly insignificant is the question, "Who is right?" Those, like Tommy and his brother, who celebrate a reconciliation day, will attest that it can be the most useless question we ask.

The Book of Genesis describes Reconciliation Day for Joseph and his brothers. Having finally revealed his identity to them, "[Joseph] kissed all his brothers and cried on each of them and then his brothers spoke with him." On their Reconciliation Day, they cried, saddened for all the time they had lost and joyful that at last they were reunited. Joseph's brothers, who "could not speak peacefully with him," in the days of their youth, spoke with him freely as he approached each one in turn. They had traveled a long and painful road to reach their Reconciliation Day. Together at last, they kissed, they cried, and they spoke—for they knew that this was one of life's most wonderful moments.

Far from being an act of weakness or a gesture of capitulation, reconciliation is a gift we give ourselves even as we offer it to someone else. It permits us to bid farewell to the thoughts which, when replayed in our minds, cast a darkness over our lives. Tomorrow never looks so good as it does to those who have released themselves from the awesome power of the past.

Reconciliation is an act of real love. This kind of love understands that disappointment and hurt are inevitable and that they can be the occasion for growth. Real love is found where people live with an awareness that, above all else, there is a treasured connection that binds them together. This connection is strong enough to survive hurt, precious enough to warrant our compassion in judgment, and more powerful than anger.

Real love is covenantal. Over time, it grows in the arena of life as people aware of shortcomings, imperfections, and transgressions commit themselves to each other. And because it is covenantal, it is mature enough to watch dreams become reduced to illusion—and yet still survive.

It is this kind of love which is described in the story told of a father who came to his rabbi and expressed his deep disappointment with his son. Troubled by the hurt his son had caused him, the father shared all his pain and bitterness with the rabbi. After telling the story, he turned to his rabbi and asked, "What shall I do now?" The rabbi's response was elegant in its simplicity. He suggested that the father go home and "love your son even more." Having gone to the rabbi seeking advice, the father left after being reminded that real love endures even when it is sorely tested.

The power of this kind of love comes across in a story told by Rabbi Jack Riemer. It is the story of a man and a teenager who shared a train ride to a place called Smithville. The man happened to sit down next to a teenage boy who was no more than 17 years old. The boy was tense and the man wondered what could be worrying somebody so young. Whatever it was, the boy's tension was clear.

The boy kept staring out the window, paying no attention to anyone else on the train. The man tried to forget about him by opening up a book and reading. But then, he would look up and see the boy's face pressed against the window. He sensed that the boy was fighting to keep from crying. This was the way that they traveled through the night—the man attempting to read and the boy sitting and staring out the window.

Finally, the boy asked the man, "Do you know what time it is? And do you know when we are due to arrive at Smithville?" The man gave the boy the time, and went on to say, "Smithville, that's a very small town, isn't it? I didn't know that the train stopped there." "It usually doesn't," said the boy. "But they said that they would stop there for me so that I could get off—if I decide to. I used to live there."

The boy returned to the window and the man to his book. It was quite a while before conversation began once again. But when it did, the boy told the man the whole story of his life. "Four years ago," he said, "I did something very bad, so bad that I had to run away from home. I couldn't face my father after what I did. So I left without even saying goodbye to him. Since then, I have worked a bit here and a bit there. I never stayed very long in one place. I've been pretty lonely. Until finally, I decided that I want to go back to my father's house."

The man went on to ask, "Does your father know that you're coming?" And the boy responded, "He knows that I'm coming, but I don't know if he will be there or not. I sent him a letter. I didn't know if he would still want me back or not after what I did. I wasn't sure if he would forgive me. So in my letter, I said that I would come home if he wanted me to. I told him that if he wanted me to come home, he could put a sign on a tree which is a few hundred yards before the railroad station in Smithville. I told him that I would look for a white ribbon on one of the branches of that tree as the train passes. If there is a white ribbon on the tree, then I'll get off. If not, then I'll just keep on riding to wherever this train goes."

A friendship developed between the man and the boy. The two of them were now waiting for Smithville. Suddenly, the boy turned to the man and asked, "Will you do me a favor? Will you please look for me? I'm scared to look for that ribbon on the tree." Now involved, the man agreed and took a turn staring out the window for a ribbon on a tree.

A few moments later, the conductor came down the aisle

and called out, "Next stop—Smithville." The boy could not move. The man, however, looked as hard as he could. And then he saw it! He shouted so loud that all the people in the train turned around. "It's there! Look, it's there! The tree is covered with white ribbons! Not just one—there's a whole bunch!"

The boy's father had every reason to reject his son. As Rabbi Riemer reflected about this story, "The father had every right and every reason not to put up a white ribbon—and yet he did." Only a father whose love is real could blanket the tree with white ribbons, each one of them proclaiming Reconciliation Day.

Some years ago, following the High Holy Days, a young woman named Vicky shared with me the story of her alienation from her mother. On several occasions, her mother had not been there when she most needed her. In times of financial emergency, her mother had turned away, leaving her to depend upon friends. Vicky said to me, "What did I need her for after that? After my mother betrayed me, our relationship changed dramatically. Though we continued to see each other, our relationship became superficial. I was determined to punish her. If she wasn't prepared to be a mother, then I wasn't going to be her daughter. I know I've hurt her and I don't want to do that anymore. Deep inside, I have a real need to show that I still love her."

Unable to approach her mother directly and speak about all that had transpired in their relationship, Vicky decided to write a letter. Several days later, she called to tell me of her mother's response. "I can't believe what my mother said. For years, she has been troubled about failing me. If there was something in her life that she could do over again, it would be the decision not to help me when I needed her. My mother said to me, 'Let's not relive the past. What matters is the two of us and our future. If we love each other, we can look beyond it all.' "

Reconciliation Day had come for Vicky and her mother, and both fully enjoyed the experience. Vicky concluded by saying, "I waited for this moment for so long. I only wish that our conversation would not end."

Vicky's words reminded me of what Shoeless Joe Jackson said to an anxious Ray Kinsella in the movie *Field of Dreams*. Ray was understandably nervous as he anticipated a reunion with his father, whom he had disappointed years ago. Seeking to calm him down, Shoeless Joe Jackson suggested to Ray that once he and his father met again, it would be like the final inning of a terrifically played game. It's a feeling that the game will go on forever.

Having found her way back to her mother, Vicky began to hope that the moment they were sharing would go on forever. Basking in the warmth of their reunion, the pains of the past began to hurt less. As they faced the future together, Vicky felt that yesterday's disappointments no longer loomed so large in her mind. Her anger began to dissipate and painful memories became hazy. No longer focusing her thoughts and her energy on the past, Vicky could look with hope to all the days yet to come. She had opened her heart to reconciliation and she was determined not to waste any more precious and irretrievable opportunities for togetherness.

When I think of Vicky and the other people I've written about, I am struck by the way their lives make real the story about the painter at the beginning of this book. Remember, his latest work was being unveiled before a gathering of art critics. They were scrutinizing the painting when one critic noticed what he felt was a glaring oversight by the artist. He called out, "Sir, I see that the door to the house in the painting has no handle. Was that deliberate?" The painter responded, "The door is the human heart. And there's no handle because it can only be opened from within."

Perhaps someone in your life is searching for the handle which will open the door to forgiveness. Perhaps there is a relative or friend hoping that your love and compassion will open the door to reunion. Perhaps, like others, you have heard a voice calling you to open the door to someone with whom you belong. My hope is that you've come to understand that only you have the power to open that door.

Charles Klein is available for speaking engagements. Please contact:

Liebling Press, Inc.
2971 Bellmore Avenue
Bellmore, NY 11710

Telephone: 516-781-8092
Telefax: 516-781-9419